# STILL LIVING?

Yeti, Sasquatch and
the Neanderthal Enigma

MYRA SHACKLEY

*with 60 illustrations*

Thames and Hudson

'The fairest thing we can experience
is the mysterious.'
Albert Einstein

Designed by Peter Bridgewater

© 1983 Myra Shackley

First published in the USA in 1983 by
Thames and Hudson Inc., 500 Fifth
Avenue, New York, New York
10110

Library of Congress Catalog Card
Number 82-50898

Printed and bound in Great Britain

# Contents

## Note on Transliteration

It is inevitable that problems with transliteration will occur when material is originally published in obscure languages, like the non-Russian dialects still written in the Cyrillic alphabet. The same author will spell his name differently when writing in different languages, and certain place-names become unfamiliar if translated directly from Ukrainian, for example. I have *tried* to be consistent and use the British Standard (BSI 2979) transliteration guidelines, and the established English equivalent of place-names, but I implore the reader's tolerance of any oversights.

# Prologue

For the last 2,500 years we have been accumulating reports of creatures which do not conform to any of our convenient zoological classifications, but which may loosely be called 'wildmen'. Initially, such reports describe only sightings, and are difficult to distinguish from myths, folklore and travellers' tales. More recently, however, the matter has been taken up by established scientists concerned with the possibility that some of the reports may refer to genuine creatures – perhaps even one or two varieties of primate (the group including both the great apes and man) and even primitive types of man. It would be difficult to overestimate the importance of such a discovery. The purpose of this book is to present not only the evidence for the existence of wildmen, but also to try to disentangle fact from fiction, the genuine article from later accretions of myth.

The character of the wildman, in one of his numerous guises, appears in the art and literature of almost every culture that has ever existed – even our own, where we use the term to imply freedom, rebellion or permissiveness. The Roman world included a wildman in the shape of the satyr, and in the Middle Ages the 'wodewose' was a convenient incarnation of ideas about a primitive way of life, a comment on society, and a central figure for allegory and romantic poetry. The very ubiquity of wildmen is suspicious, and there is considerable similarity between themes and characters in the mythology of peoples widely separated in space and time. Many theories have been evolved to account for this. Allowing for the presence in every society of occasional genuine 'monsters' – giants, genetic freaks[1] and so on – it is possible to argue that all wildman stories are merely myths (and therefore untrue), and that societies borrow the myths from each other, as was certainly the case with Greece and Rome. But it is difficult to account for the fact that similar stories appear in different continents, unless you postulate

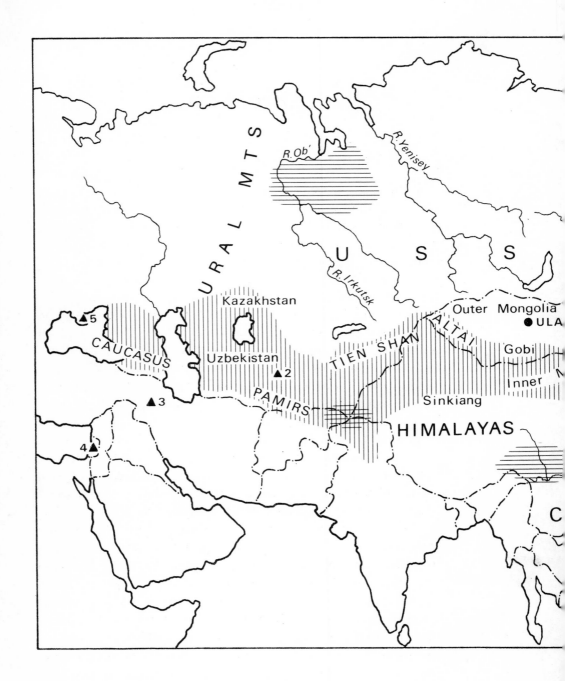

1 The main areas where Yetis, Almas and Chuchunaa have been sighted. The overlap between sightings of Almas and known Neanderthal sites is striking. (1) Sjara-osso-gol (Inner Mongolia); (2) Teshik-Tash

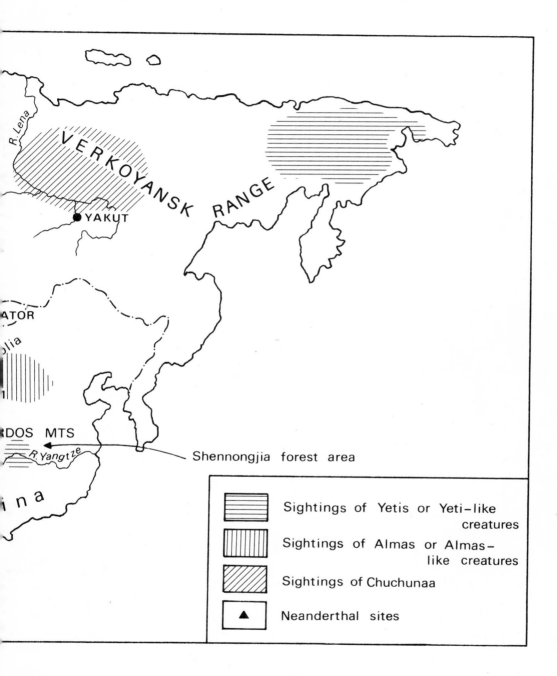

*(Uzbekistan); (3) Shanidar (Iraq); (4); Mount Carmel caves (Israel); (5) Kiik-koba and Starosel'e (Crimea).*

some common heartland from which the stories diffused, an idea contrary to modern anthropological thinking. Another possibility, however, is that all societies create wildmen because outside their own inhabited or explored territories there always lie unfamiliar regions, which hearsay and travellers' tales will populate with strange, unidentified creatures. Some of these creatures will be mythical, the product of the vivid human imagination, but others may be based on genuine sightings of unknown and unclassified species. Chapter 1 examines the hazy picture from the distant past, and asks whether any of the creatures possibly surviving today can be traced back into history. The rest of this book takes the more solid evidence of sightings in modern times or the recent past to see if a case can be made for the existence of authentic living wildmen – and if so, to diagnose who or what they may be.

In his *Systema Naturae* of 1775, which introduced biological nomenclature as we know it today, the great Swedish zoologist Carl Linnaeus identified not just one species of living man (ourselves, *Homo sapiens*) but several, including 'wildman' (*Homo ferus*) and a primitive man, *Homo troglodytes* ('cave man'), which were classified together with modern man and living apes under the general heading of primates. Linnaeus based his conclusions on reports made by ancient authors and travellers, but the idea that other, more primitive varieties of man could have survived and still exist in the modern world did not find favour – indeed was actively ridiculed – until 200 years later. Since the 1950s, however, scientists have been undergoing a change of heart, thanks to new discoveries in the field of human evolution.

The first fossil finds of an early and supposedly more primitive form of man were made as long ago as 1856, in the Neander valley near Düsseldorf, which gave its name to the new species – Neanderthal man.[2] At first the remains were thought to be those of a Mongol or an idiot, but gradually further evidence, including the discovery of their ancestor, an even more primitive 'hominid' (manlike creature) – *Homo erectus* – led to the acceptance of a lengthy and complex evolution for man. The question became – how lengthy and how complex? Neanderthal man, our immediate predecessor, had a brain size and upright stance fully comparable with that of modern man – indeed eventually he was classified as a subspecies of *Homo sapiens, Homo sapiens neanderthalensis* (we ourselves are now classified as *Homo sapiens sapiens*). But did he evolve directly into us? His barrel chest, long, low-vaulted skull, heavy brow ridges, receding chin and prominent jaw would all suggest that he did not. But if not, what happened to him after 30,000 years ago, when his remains disappear from the fossil record and those of modern man take over? Did he just die out?

The fate of the Neanderthals, arguably one of the most interesting problems in all prehistory, has provoked heated debate and scholarly discussion for decades. Some people believe that a few Neanderthals could in fact have survived – might they be what Linnaeus called 'wildmen'? This attractive hypothesis caught the imagination of the greatest name in wildman studies, the late Russian Professor Boris Porshnev. In the face of much ridicule and opposition, he attempted to demonstrate in numerous publications over a period of thirty years that some of the sightings of hairy manlike creatures referred to hominid survivals ('relict hominids'), in particular to surviving Neanderthals. His most accessible work on the subject, written with another wildman expert, Bernard Heuvelmans, was published in Paris in 1974 under the title *L'homme de néanderthal est toujours vivant*.[3] Porshnev's ideas received a boost in the 1960s and 1970s from the discovery that human evolution has been infinitely more complex than was once thought. Finds made in East Africa show that there is no longer a clear, unilinear evolutionary chain for man. It seems that at several stages in human development over the last 5 million years a number of closely related species coexisted: among others, the hominids *Australopithecus africanus*, *A. robustus* and *Homo habilis* overlapped between 3 million and 2 million years ago, and *Homo habilis* overlapped with *Homo erectus* around $1\frac{1}{2}$ million years ago. If that was true for millions of years, why should it not be true today – why is it so unlikely that Neanderthal man still lives?

In 1958, largely as a result of Porshnev's work, the Academy of Sciences of the USSR organized what became known as the famous 'Snowman Commission', set up to examine all the reports of manlike creatures, correlate them, analyze them and produce some serious hypotheses. An expedition was mounted to the Pamir mountains in southern Russia, and accounts from eye-witnesses were recorded across the length and breadth of the country. Although the results were inconclusive, and marked the end of the short period of official Russian involvement in the problem, they did with hindsight indicate a startling fact – that there might be at least two, if not three, unknown and unclassified manlike or apelike creatures residing in the remote mountains and plateaux of the Soviet Union.

One of the creatures was apparently already well known from other parts of Asia, more particularly the eastern Himalayas. This was the apelike Yeti, popularized in the Western world as the 'Abominable Snowman' and sighted sporadically by travellers and climbers in the mountains of Nepal since the 1920s. Soviet reports indicated a scattered distribution for the Russian Yeti – if such it was – from easternmost and westernmost Siberia in the north to the Pamirs in the south. But in addition reports were coming in from the Pamirs as well as Outer Mongolia, the Caucasus and elsewhere that there existed a more manlike wildman (here and throughout for convenience given its Mongolian name, the Almas).[4] Apparently much shorter and less hairy than the Yeti, some accounts credited the Almas with a heavily built but human-like frame and face combined with tool-using ability. Might this be Porshnev's Neanderthal survivor? Matters were further complicated by sightings of taller, even more manlike, wildmen in a limited area of northeast Siberia around Yakut, where the creatures were known as Chuchunaa.

Interest in the possible existence of living wildmen was not confined to the Soviet Union or travellers to Nepal. In North America there had been occasional newspaper reports of large, hairy ape- or manlike creatures since the 19th century, and during the 1950s and 1960s a large number of accounts appeared purporting to demonstrate the presence there of a tall wildman called Bigfoot or the Sasquatch. Sightings, footprints, hairs and droppings came from a wide area, centring on the remote coniferous forest mountain regions of the Pacific Northwest, stretching from northern California in the south to British Columbia in the north. Estimates of size, shape and way of life seemed to suggest interesting links with the Asian Yeti. A celebrated piece of film, shot by Roger Patterson while trekking in northern California in 1967, caused widespread interest, because it apparently showed a female Sasquatch – a crucial piece of evidence if genuine, since no other photographs or film of wildmen, living or dead, have yet been obtained. But, like most things to do with Bigfoot, the tremendous publicity surrounding the whole episode served merely to cloud the issues involved. The publicity has nevertheless resulted in increased funding for Bigfoot enquiries, and centres for serious Sasquatch research have been set up which, together with the sheer wealth of accumulated data, are persuading many scientists that Bigfoot is something more than simply a piece of folklore.

The same cannot be said for the extremely slender evidence of a more manlike creature in North America. The case largely depends on giving credence to the so-called 'Iceman', a creature displayed completely frozen within a block of ice in an insulated coffin, and first examined by scientists in 1968 while it resided on a farm in Minnesota, after a strenuous tour of American carnivals. It had, so the owner claimed initially, been found floating in an enormous block of ice in the Sea of Okhotsk off the coast of eastern Siberia by either Russian sealers or Japanese whalers (depending on which story you believed). Eventually it arrived in Hong Kong and was purchased for exhibition in the United States at 35 cents a look, only to start a long and incredibly complicated saga about its authenticity and disputed provenance. Two experts in hominid studies, Ivan T. Sanderson and Bernard Heuvelmans, measured and examined it as best they could through the block of ice, and Heuvelmans convinced himself that it was genuine, and moreover a genuine deep-frozen Neanderthal.[5] The first reports suggested to at least one eminent anatomist, however, that the Iceman combined the worst features of an ape and a man in a way that was most unlikely at our present state of knowledge about human evolution. And, indeed, the original Iceman mysteriously disappeared before scientists from the prestigious Smithsonian Institution could examine it, being replaced by a so-called 'model'. The scope for hoaxers, confidence-tricksters or just plain storytellers in the field of wildman studies is enormous, and one needs to be constantly on one's guard in the search for authentic observations amongst the

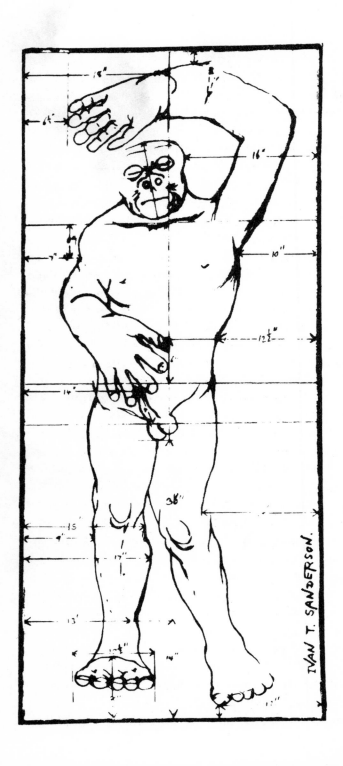

welter of reports, whether from America, Russia or anywhere else.

For reliable information about wildman research in the Soviet Union in recent years, scientists in the West are greatly indebted to Porshnev's heir, Dmitri Bayanov of the Darwin Museum, Moscow. An informal seminar was started at the museum in 1960 to discuss current wildman research and reports by scholars, travellers, climbers and geographers from all over Asia. The seminars are currently chaired by Bayanov with the cooperation of his colleague, Igor Burtsev. Reports from this source indicate that there were a number of quite successful Russian expeditions to regions such as the Caucasus and the Pamirs in the 1960s and 1970s. Some of the most exciting new evidence, however, comes not from the Soviet Union but from China, where in the 1970s and 1980s sightings have been recorded of a Yeti-like creature in the remote mountainous region of Shennongjia forest, Hubei province. Together with other rare or unique flora and fauna, such as the dove tree and the white bear, the Yeti might survive there. The Chinese have mounted large-scale expeditions to find out the truth, and an area of Shennongjia forest has been designated as a Yeti reserve.

The time has now come to take a close look at the mass of evidence for living wildmen in order to see whether a convincing pattern emerges. Do the Yeti, Almas, Chuchunaa and Bigfoot truly exist, or are they in reality based on nothing more elaborate than folktales, woven around half-seen creatures of known origin? If they do exist, what are they? How many of them survive, and where? Could any of them be relict hominids, survivors from the distant past of human and primate evolution? Boris Porshnev fervently believed not only that relict hominids exist today, but that their ancestors can be found in the satyrs, centaurs and fauns of the classical pantheon of antiquity, and we should begin by examining his ideas and the evidence for other ancient as well as medieval wildmen.

2 *Drawing of the 'Iceman' by Ivan T. Sanderson. Probably a brilliant fake of latex rubber, this 'hominid' was supposedly killed by a gunshot wound and then found enclosed in a block of ice as a fairground exhibit.*

# Chapter 1
# Wildmen–
# Ancient and Modern

If wildmen exist today in the form of Yetis or Almas or the Chuchunaa, can we find evidence for their more widespread distribution in the past in the writings of ancient and medieval authors? The wildman, in various manifestations, forms part of the culture and mythology of almost every society since records began, but the problem we face is – how to distinguish myth from reality?

The further back in time one goes, the more difficult it becomes to disentangle fact from fiction – particularly since such distinctions were rarely important to ancient peoples themselves. The earliest wildman to appear in literature can be found in the Epic of Gilgamesh, which may well have been built around an actual king of that name in southern Babylonia. He must have been a man of considerable personality since he became associated with numerous stories, combined in the form of this short epic around 2000 B C. The stories, recorded on twelve imperfect tablets, were found in the Assurbanipal library in the ruins of Nineveh, tablets which also contained an account of the Biblical Flood.

Gilgamesh seems to have been two-thirds a god, and also a powerful king and mighty warrior. One day, so the legend goes, Arura the potter washed his hands, pinched clay and made the wildman Enkidu, who was shaggy with 'hair that sprouted like grain', and who ate with the gazelles and drank with the wild beasts at their waterholes. The first hunter to encounter him was so frightened that he dared not approach, and let the animals he was hunting go free. Eventually a hunter went to Gilgamesh the king with a request for help, and the king recommended that he take a priestess of Ishtar with him to the waterhole and instruct her to take off her clothes, thus enticing poor Enkidu away from his animal friends. The ruse succeeded and the wildman enjoyed her favours for a week, being gradually persuaded to eat bread and drink wine with the shepherds. He became their friend and helped them by driving lions away from the flocks, until the priestess tempted him by boasting of the greatness of Gilgamesh, hinting that the king alone was worthy of being Enkidu's rival or friend. Inevitably the two champions met and after a titanic battle Gilgamesh won, but Enkidu received his respect and undying friendship. The wildman is then seen fighting at the king's side against a monster (Humbaba), and the two become inseparable companions until Enkidu is mortally wounded. At his deathbed Gilgamesh cries for him – 'like a wailing woman I cry for Enkidu my friend, What now to me are my festal robe, my axe, my lance, my sword?' – and on his death the king roars like a lion and tears the hair from his head before going into six days of mourning. Leaving aside this lavish expression of grief, the important thing seems to be that Gilgamesh viewed the wildman Enkidu as a *man*, saying: 'My friend, who endured all hardships with me, has been overtaken by the fate of mankind'.

We must interpret the wildman legends and mythology within the framework of the cultures which created them, resisting the temptation to impose our own values. There are, however, considerable similarities between themes, characters and even details in the mythology of cultures very widely separated in time and space and many theories have been evolved to account for this.

Carl Jung, for instance, argued that a 'collective unconscious' was responsible for the fact that the myths, symbols and fairy tales of many cultures show dramatic similarities. The French anthropologist Claude Lévi-Strauss, on the other hand, believes the myths pass from person to person and culture to culture; though they may undergo transformations, they retain the same structural principles.

A more likely possibility is that different primitive peoples, faced with the same situations and natural phenomena, ask the same questions and tend to answer them in the same way. Thus, since most cultures have a territorial concept which involves extensive 'badlands' – wild places outside the limits of their civilization – it is natural that these uninhabited areas should be populated by a rich variety of mythological creatures, some totally imaginary but others related to known species. The difficulty lies in distinguishing which is which: is the wildman of legend purely mythological or is he based on some half-forgotten prototype?

It is important to remember, for instance, how limited was the
experience of classical historians and geographers; during the 1st
century A D Pliny in his *Natural History* refers to *silvestres*
('woodland creatures') which are hairy with yellow eyes, canine
teeth, no speech but horrible shrieks. Not relict hominids, one
suspects, but probably gibbons. The historian Herodotus (5th
century B C) talks of hairy monsters in Libya, and there is a very
garbled account of gorillas in Sierra Leone by the writer Pomponius
Mela in the 1st century A D. Much confusion existed in the Roman
mind about the precise status of these vaguely human-looking
creatures, and no formal distinction between any of the different
varieties of primate was ever made. Nor was anyone clear about
how mankind itself could be accounted for, or what distinctions
must be made between man, wildman and other primates. Were
they all varieties of the same creature?

## Satyrs, centaurs and fauns

In the Greek and Roman imagination the wildman usually took the
form of a satyr, half man, half beast, often equipped with horns and
tail and generally depicted undertaking some form of erotic
activity. The satyr figure, invented by Athenian artists by 580 B C, is
one of the most frequently represented in the extensive mythological repertoire of the classical world, and possibly its most
engaging component. Boris Porshnev, with his customary thorough-
ness, made a careful examination of Greek and Roman art and
literature for possible references to relict hominids, assuming that
the existence of such creatures would certainly have been recorded
somewhere, somehow. He hit upon the satyr with delight, claiming
that here, at last, in the extensive series of satyr paintings and the
numerous references to satyrs and their companions in all forms of
classical literature, was the proof that wildmen (relict hominids)
still existed in Roman times.

In Greek mythology the role of satyrs changes with time; at first
they are no more than wild superhuman beings with which fancy
and imagination peopled mountains and forests. Then they become
associated with the god of wine, Dionysus, and because of their
affinity with him they enter his train and become his regular

companions. Their perpetual cheerful tumescence symbolizes freedom and the pleasures of the good life. By the end of the 6th century B C the first satyr plays appear in Athens, with actors dressed as satyrs armed with large, flexible phalli. In later dramas scenes occur which are often parodies of the earlier myths, and satyrs act out moral fantasies in a manner exactly analogous to medieval wildman plays.

J.D. Beazley's great works on Greek vase painting[1] show satyrs on almost every page. They are always depicted with a combination of human and animal characteristics – a horse's tail, for example, together with a human shape, snub nose and savage profile. They have straight, pointed goat-like ears, bald foreheads and long, flowing beards. Two distinct types seem to have been painted; one is thin and nervous-looking and drawn with a clean dry outline (fig. 3), while the other is puffy, the result of too much drink, sensual and rather bloated. These seem to be the only sort that are ever shown with substantial amounts of hair. *Really* hairy satyrs are very rare indeed, and are painted by the appropriately-named 'Painter of the Woolly Satyrs'. Greek art also shows *sileni*, comic, older satyrs with fat, hairy limbs, fur vests and full wineskins.

The often-reproduced illustration of a supposed 'hominid' making friends with a human being (fig. 4) from a Greek vase actually shows a very typical satyr of the second variety approaching a wine vessel from which some minor deity is obligingly removing the lid. Vase painters represented satyrs in the traditional way for some time, but by the 4th century B C sculptors had developed a new sort of satyr called a 'faun', a title retained in Roman mythology.[2] Few of the animal characteristics of the satyr remained, only the pointed ears and faunskin over the shoulder giving a clue to the statue's origins, although the figure was usually equipped with a fleshy gland under the chin and little sprouting horns. It is generally shown drunk, and often laughing maniacally.

Greek art is remarkable for the very small number of demonic figures ever represented, and the form of the satyr was devised by artists at a relatively late date.[3] Had the satyr been based on some genuine wildman or hominid quite the opposite might have been expected, and we should see a progression from very realistic satyrs

3 *Often called an 'aggressive hominid', but actually a conventional satyr holding a branch or rattle. Carthaginian or Phoenician bowl, 7th century BC.*

to figures with more mythological characteristics. The earliest Greek literary references suggest that at first the satyr was merely a lazy country demon with no specific function, and it would be all too easy to be misled by the later representations into believing that they incorporate the original essence of the creature involved. The same really applies to centaurs, who were not horse-like at all in the earliest Greek stories. The Porshnev theory, which saw satyrs, fauns, *sileni* and nymphs as different ways of depicting surviving hominids, seems to receive no support from classical art or literature.

R obert Graves, certainly the greatest living authority on Greek mythology, sees the satyrs as representing actual goat-totem tribesmen, followers of the woodland god Pan, and the centaurs as horse-totem tribesmen who worshipped the drunken god Dionysus.[4] In both cases he suggests that the rites involved drug

4 *Furry satyr approaching a wine vessel from which a nymph is obligingly removing the lid. Greek vase painting.*

intoxication using the mushroom *Amanita muscaria* (fly agaric), which induces hallucinations, senseless rioting, prophetic sight, erotic energy and remarkable strength – all the characteristics, in fact, which are habitually attributed to the satyrs and centaurs of classical mythology.[5] The connection between drug-taking and the worship of the ancient gods, including Pan, is far from extinct and survives today in white witchcraft or magic.

## Medieval wildmen[6]

Most of the European literary material dealing with the wildman dates from the 12th century onwards, with visual representations occurring from the mid-13th century. His greatest period of popularity was undoubtedly after 1350, gradually dying away at different times in different areas with the exception of some of the more remote regions, where belief in a wildman is still common today.

Attitudes towards, and images of, the wildman altered with time. In the early medieval period he was simply a pagan idea, a continuation of the old Graeco-Roman forest creatures and demigods; but later on he became a reflection of the medieval concern with allegory, status and religion. The wildman stories have a corollary in the undoubted existence of a wildman cult, which produced the core of ritual and myth to be elaborated by storytellers and depicted by artists.

Medieval wildmen were generally hairy, with both human and animal traits. Often they were covered with fur, except for the face, feet and hands. They frequently carried a club or mace and were sometimes depicted wearing a leaf kilt. Some were manlike but others took their place in bestiaries – on the earliest European card game known, for example, the wildmen are bracketed with plants and beasts. Their nature and character could change too as secondary characteristics were added or subtracted (a tail perhaps, or a pair of horns), thus transforming them into devils, fauns or satyrs. Posture could also help define the degree of wildness. Upright posture meant that the figure was human, and wildmen (for example, the one in plate 7, who is supposed to be Nebuchadnezzar in the wild state) were sometimes shown on all fours to emphasize the animal nature of their affliction. But in Spenser's *Faerie Queene* the wildman has a noble ancestry – therefore he is human. Other accounts of wildmen clearly refer to lunatics, and still others to imaginary beings.

For the medieval peasant the wildman was simultaneously an allegorical figure, the centre of a cult, the real or legendary inhabitant of wild places and a traditional figure. These ideas cannot be separated.[7] One thing he does *not* seem to have been perceived as is a primitive type of man, in the sense of a relict hominid.[8]

Certain traits were common to many areas and many myths of the wildman. He was usually incapable of speech and unable to recognize the existence of God – a catastrophe to the medieval mind. His diet was different in different accounts, but was principally composed of berries, acorns and raw animal flesh, reflecting the solitary nature of his existence. Wildmen were outside society both physically, because they lived beyond its boundaries, and socially, because they observed none of its conventions, either secular or religious. Thus any place outside civilization could, potentially, be the home of the wildman. Caves were especially favoured, as was the deep forest.

The wildwoman, who is referred to only rarely and even less often depicted, is sometimes found where no wildman myths have ever been, or where they have been allowed to fade out, and she seems to have had a wider range of habitat, extending out of the mountains and forests and into the plains. Some wildwomen have long breasts which they throw over their shoulders (this is a common folklore theme), while others are small and modest, called wood or moss damsels. Sometimes the wildwoman is recognized as a witch, and there are strong erotic connotations here, since such witches are often thought to crave mortal men. They occasionally materialize in dreams, and in 1691 a young man in Sweden was condemned to death for having had carnal relationships with just such a wildwoman (a *skogra*), providing an indication of how strong these traditions might be, and how late they survived.

Although the wildman appears in an enormous range of medieval literature, he does *not* seem to occur in contemporary letters or semi-official documents, not even in the medieval *exemplar* stories for preaching which are compounded of folklore and classic tales of sometimes ancient origin.[9] If the medieval wildman had indeed been based on an original living prototype surely at least *one* reference in these non-fictional sources would have survived?

Wildmen are important figures in medieval paintings and illuminated manuscripts. They may be called 'wodewoses' or 'woodhouses', and are frequently shown covered with long hair or fur. An additional class of picture shows actors in plays, masques and dramas who are depicted in wildman costumes. A recent survey[10] of wildman representations from the 8th to the 16th centuries produced many examples which mirror the way in which the wildman is portrayed in literature. Although apes and monkeys can be clearly distinguished as well as wildmen, it is not possible to identify other varieties of primate. The name 'wodewose' is derived from the Anglo-Saxon *Wudewasa* and thence from *Wudu* (late Old English for a wood); *Wudewasa* seems to mean 'man-of-the-wood', although it can also mean 'savage', 'satyr', 'faun', and later on was used as well for anyone dressed like a wildman in a play or pageant. Ivan Sanderson, who completed this survey, believes that after the 16th century the memory of genuine (hominid) early wodewoses became dimmed and that much confusion existed between this folk memory and accounts of newly-discovered primates in the tropics. However, wodewoses were still to be found in Europe until the 15th century, and there is a vivid example of a hairy wildman attacking (and being attacked by) dogs in the 14th-century Queen Mary's Psalter now in the British Library (fig. 5).

I believe that wodewoses are a continuation of the classical satyr mythology. The fact that representations of them change over time merely indicates changes in the role of the wildman within the cult that had grown up around him, not a progression from an original prototype post-Roman wodewose whose representations became more and more degenerate. The wodewose is an imaginary being, differing from the satyr only in the lack of a tail and the frequent addition of a large club, but still essentially a creature of legend. The fact that he is often shown in association with other mythical beasts seems to clinch the matter.

5 *Wildman chasing dogs. From a 14th-century drollery in 'Queen Mary's Psalter'.*

The wildman (who may be the same as the 'green man') also takes on the role of the spirit of the woods, a kind of pagan nature god, a reaction against claustrophobic Christian rituals. His image permeates every form of medieval art, from architecture to heraldry, and in the latter he is often shown as a supporter of an armorial shield. Over 200 European families have wildmen as heraldic emblems, and many more as supporters. Any nude figure in heraldry is called a 'savage', 'wildman' or 'woodman', and the terms are quite interchangeable. There is little variation in the way they are portrayed, leafy decorations and a club being the rule. Many members of the English nobility have a coat of arms which includes such figures, and that of Earl Poulett (fig. 6) has a male *and* female 'savage' (the only example known where both occur together).

Wildmen (or green men) also appear carved in wood and as architectural adornments in the Middle Ages, and are very common on bench-ends and misericords. Green men are frequently shown as a face with foliage emerging from the mouth, and fifty or more of these are known from England alone.[11] The green man is also found carved in stone, as a gargoyle or an architectural ornament.

In the Elizabethan period wildmen, or green men, were often employed to clear the way for processions, wielding sticks. In pageants they fought dragons and were favourite popular characters. They also occur on English inn signs, although the appellation 'The Green Man' may alternatively be derived from a forester (from

6 *Coat of arms of Earl Poulett, with male and female wildmen as supporters, from* Burkes Peerage.

the 17th century onwards) who was usually dressed in green, and is connected with Robin Hood who dressed in Lincoln (or Kendal) green.[12]

The depiction of the wildman in dances and pageants is interesting and lasted for a very long time. The actor playing a wildman was more than just an actor, he was regarded as the living recipient of wildman power; by dressing up as a wildman he *became* a wildman in a manner exactly paralleled on the other side of the world, where actors portray Yetis in Tibetan ritual dance-drama. The most famous pictorial representation of a pageant with a wildman is certainly that of Bruegel the Elder, in the *Battle of Carnival and Lent*, where the emperor and his followers are closing in on one poor wildman dressed in green who is being led by a female figure with a ring (fig. 7). The play, apparently being enacted by a small group of players, is typical of the genre which depicts classic wildman legends, the hunt, the finding of a wildman in the mountains or his rescue by a princess.

We have come a long way from the simple wildman lurking in remote woodlands of the Middle Ages, but we are still in the realms

7 *Wildman in a play, the Masquerade of Valentine and Orson. A 16th-century Flemish print after Pieter Bruegel the Elder.*

of fantasy and imagination. Until proved otherwise the European wildman, whether he is called a wodewose, a green man, a satyr or anything else, remains a creature of legend. It is possible that genuine relict hominids were sighted from time to time somewhere in the world during the Middle Ages, but *verbatim* descriptions have not survived. The European wildman is a myth, becoming increasingly elaborate with time, but quite in keeping with the folklore and traditions of the period.

## Feral Children

The legendary Romulus and Remus were reared by a wolf, and ever since their day there have been numerous accounts of 'feral' children – children brought up in the wild, away from humanity. Some of these accounts are clearly fictitious, but others appear to be factual. Lucien Malson, in his book *Les Enfant Sauvages* (1974), lists fifty-three cases of feral children since 1344, ending with the discovery of a boy in the jungle of Sri Lanka in 1973, who had apparently been brought up by monkeys.[13] There seems little doubt that children have at various times and in various places lived successfully for a period in the wild.

But do any of the accounts genuinely describe children reared by animals, or – even more speculatively – relict hominid children? Again one is presented with the problem of distinguishing fact from fiction, or at least of knowing how to interpret supposed fact. For instance, in the case of the famous Indian wolf children, rescued by the Reverend J.A.L. Singh in 1920 from a wolves' lair near Midanpore, there was an indisputable association between wolf and children, attested by many eye-witnesses (wolves have a highly organized social structure, and are the 'parents' in three-quarters of reported cases).[14] But at what age had the children begun to live with the wolves? Could they really have survived the early years after weaning, or were they actually found only a few days after their loss?

Many of the accounts do not mention any liaison with animal 'parents', for example the following passage, which tells of the discovery of a wild girl in 1767 by the inhabitants of Fraumark in Lower Hungary when pursuing a bear in the mountains:[15]

... came to a cave in the rocks in which a completely naked wild girl was found. She was tall, robust, and seemed to be about eighteen years old. Her skin was very brown and she looked frightened. Her behaviour was very crude. They had to use violence to make her leave the cave. But she did not cry and did not shed any tears. Finally they succeeded in bringing her to Karpfen, a small town in the county of Atlsohl, where she was locked up in an Asylum. She would only eat raw meat . . .

This is clearly an early account of the finding of a feral child, but with no indication that the child had been adopted by animals nor

that it was anything except a backward specimen of *Homo sapiens.*
Both this and the following account of the discovery of a wildman[16]
have been taken by some writers to support the case for hominid
survival in Europe. They seem to me to be tales of the finding of
unfortunate persons who might have been suffering from some
form of mental deficiency.

According to Roy, in the Pyrenees, shepherds who herded their
flocks in the wood of Ivary saw a wild man in the year 1774, who
lived in a cleft in the rocks. He appeared to be about thirty years of
age, was very tall with hair like that of a bear, who could run as
quickly as a chamois. He appeared to be bright and happy and
according to appearances was not ungently in character. He never
had anything to do with anyone, and had no apparent interest in so
doing. He often came near to the huts of the shepherds without
making an attempt to take anything. Milk, bread, and cheese
appeared to be unknown things to him, for he would not even take
them when they were placed in his way. His greatest pleasure was to
frighten the sheep, and break up the herds.

This is one of a number of descriptions of individuals who for some
reason or other wished to live apart from society, or were prevented
from doing so.[17] Since societies tend to look askance at those who
reject their values and customs for whatever reason, such solitaries
either came to be regarded as idiots or were endowed with magical
powers, especially if they were female. The social pressure to
reintroduce feral children to civilized life was strong. The 'wolf
child' of Hesse, for example, discovered in 1344 after having lived in
the forest with wolves for four years, was incapable of moving
except on all fours, so his legs were then strapped to boards to 'help'
him assume normal human posture. Feral children, when restored
to civilization, were seldom able to learn more than a few words and
usually died after a short period. One exception is the case of a boy
found in the forests of Aveyron (central France) in 1799, after
having been lost when meandering in the woods some years
before (fig. 8).[18] He had survived by eating nuts and berries and liked
the life, since he escaped his well-meaning captors. After a short
period of freedom he was eventually recaptured and examined by a
leading psychologist, to be diagnosed as an incurable idiot. A
stroke of good fortune followed when the boy, named Victor, came
under the care of Jean-Marc Itard, a teacher in a deaf-and-dumb

8 *The wild boy of Aveyron, pulled out of a tree in central France by hunters in 1799. He became a textbook case of re-education.*

school with a surprisingly advanced curriculum. Victor lived to almost forty, apparently an agreeable and appealing character. Recently he became the subject of François Truffaut's enchanting film, *L'Enfant Sauvage* (1970).

Current research is beginning to confound those who doubted children's ability to survive long periods in the wild, or the likelihood of their ever having been brought up by animals. Observations have been made of the behaviour of feral children while they were still in contact with their animal protectors. For instance, the French anthropologist Jean-Claude Armen in 1974 published an account of the so-called 'gazelle boy' of the Sahara,[19] whose behaviour was completely integrated with that of the gazelle herd with whom he was living, down to minute details of posture and movement. The child was neither mentally subnormal nor abnormal (despite claims that all feral children are mental defectives).[20] Other authenticated cases have come to light including two 'gazelle boys' in North Africa, a seven-year-old ape boy from the Central African republic of Burundi, and another ape boy living in the jungle of Sri Lanka discovered in 1974.[21]

But none of the accounts of feral children seem genuinely to refer to relict hominids, not even the most detailed of all the stories, which comes from what is now Rumania and is quoted by Bayanov and Burtsev of the Darwin Museum as the ultimate proof of relict hominid survival. The original account was written down in 1796, only two years after the child had last been seen, but appears in subsequent compendia:

Here you have information about the wild boy who was found a few years ago in the Siebenbürgen-Wallachischen border [Rumania] and was brought to Kronstadt [now Braşov], where in 1784 he is still alive. How the poor boy was saved from the forests . . . I cannot tell. However one must preserve the facts, as they are, in the sad gallery of pictures of this kind.

This unfortunate youth was of the male sex and was of medium size. He had an extremely wild glance. His eyes lay deep in his head, and rolled around in a wild fashion. His forehead was strongly bent inwards, and his hair of ash-gray colour grew out short and rough. He had heavy brown eyebrows, which projected out far over his eyes, and a small flat-pressed nose. His neck appeared puffy, and at the windpipe he appeared goitrous. His mouth stood somewhat out when he held it half open as he generally did since he breathed through his mouth. His tongue was almost motionless, and his cheeks appeared more hollow than full and, like his face, were covered with a dirty yellowish skin. On the first glance at his face, from which a wildness and a sort of animal-being shone forth, one felt that it belonged to no rational creature. . . . The other parts of the wild boy's body, especially the back and the chest, were very hairy; the muscles on his arms and legs were stronger and more visible than on ordinary people. The hands were marked with callouses . . . on the fingers he had very long nails; and, on the elbows and knees, he had knobbly hardenings. The toes were longer than ordinary. He walked erect, but a little heavily. . . . He carried his head and chest forward. . . . He walked barefooted and did not like shoes on his feet. He was completely lacking in speech. . . . The sounds which he uttered were ununderstandable murmuring, which he would give when his guard drove him ahead of him. This murmuring was increased to a howling when he saw woods or even a tree. . . . When I saw him the first time, he had no sense of possession. Probably it was his complete unfamiliarity with his new condition, and the longing for his earlier life in the wilds, which he displayed when he saw a garden or a wood. . . . Aside from the original human body which usually causes a pitiful impression in this state of wildness, and aside from walking erect, one missed in him all the characteristic traits through which human beings are distinguished from the animals. . . . In the beginning his food consisted only of all kinds of tree leaves, grass, roots, and raw meat . . . according to the saying of the person who took care of him, a whole year passed before he learned to eat cooked food; when very obviously his animal wildness diminished.

I am unable to say how old he was. Outwardly he could have been from twenty-three to twenty-five years old. Probably he will never learn how to speak. When I saw him again after three years, I still found him speechless, though changed very obviously in many other respects. His face still expressed something animal-like but had become softer. . . . The desire for food, of which he now liked all kinds (particularly legumes), he would show by intelligible sounds. . . . He had gotten used to wear shoes and other clothes; but he was careless about how much they were torn. Slowly he was able to find a way to his house without a leader; the only work for which he could be used consisted of giving him a water jug which he would fill at the well and bring it to the house. . . . The instinct of imitation was shown on many occasions; but nothing made a permanent impression on him. Even if he imitated a thing several times he soon forgot it again, except the custom which had to do with his natural needs, such as eating, drinking, sleeping, etc. . . . He showed his likeness with a child in the fact that he would gape at everything which one showed to him; but, with the same lack of concentration, he would change his glance from the old objects to new ones. If one showed him a mirror he would look behind it for the image before him. But he was completely indifferent when he did not find it, and would allow the mirror to get out of his range of vision. The tunes from musical instruments seemed to interest him a little, but it was a very slight interest which did not leave any impression. . . . Since 1784, the year he left Kronstadt, I never had a chance to receive any more reports about him.[22]

For me, this is a classic description of a feral child (although the boy could have been as old as twenty-five), with a suggestion of pronounced mental deficiency. It is tempting to read phrases such as 'his forehead was strongly bent inwards' or 'the muscles on his arms and legs were stronger and more visible than on ordinary people', and identify characteristics of a relict hominid. But the evidence is simply not strong enough for us to be able to make such an identification confidently. The report is unique for its great detail, and most unlikely to have been invented. This takes us no further, however, in our quest for a more widespread distribution of wildmen – relict hominids – in former times.

Although the historical description of wildmen cannot be said to support a theory of relict hominids, every so often one comes upon such a vivid and detailed description that one must consider the possibility that it is based on fact. In this passage from *De Rerum Natura* (1st century B C), Lucretius is describing a race of earth-born men who were

built up on larger and more solid bones within, fastened with strong sinews traversing the flesh; not easily to be harmed by heat or cold or strange food or any taint of the body. . . . Nor as yet did they know how to serve their purposes with fire, nor to use skins and clothe their body in the spoils of wild beasts, but dwelt in woods and the caves on mountains and forests, and amid brushwood would hide their rough limbs, when constrained to shun the shock of winds and the rain-showers. . . . And like bristly boars these woodland men would lay their limbs naked on the ground, when overtaken by night time, wrapping themselves up around with leaves and foliage.

This is an uncannily accurate description of prehistoric man as revealed by modern archaeology. The detail in the report certainly seems to suggest that it is based on fact. But whether Lucretius was describing relict hominids or simply a backward race of anatomically modern men it is hard to determine.

As we turn now to more recent accounts of wildmen, we will be looking not only for equal vividness and realism, but also for similarities among the stories. If we are even to admit the possible existence of surviving hominids, the accounts will have to meet the tests of frequency and coherence.

# Chapter 2
# Bigfoot in North America

All too often researchers declare that either the North American Sasquatch (Bigfoot) exists or it is the best and most complicated hoax in history. In fact there is a strong possibility that both statements are partially true. Even convinced Sasquatch sceptics are weakening in the face of a rapidly expanding body of evidence for the giant-sized primate, including over a thousand sightings by both American Indian and white hunters, trappers, and many others; reports, photographs and casts of tracks (including one of a crippled Sasquatch); faeces and hair found near the tracks, tapes of Bigfoot vocalizations; and a large body of Indian folklore related to the subject. Last, but by no means least, there is a famous film made by Roger Patterson apparently of a female Sasquatch.

In the face of all this evidence it may seem difficult to understand how anyone could still remain in doubt; but there are three good reasons why the case for Bigfoot sounds simpler than it is. Firstly, much of the evidence is ambiguous and there is no question that some of it, if only a small amount, is indeed faked. Secondly, there is the reluctance of many people to envisage the possibility that large unclassified primates could be lurking in the woods of civilized America, even though most of the reports come from the heavily forested and uninhabited regions of the Pacific Northwest, extending from northern California in the south to British Columbia in the north. The third major problem is that the Sasquatch has been subjected to the relentless attentions of the press and the media, with the result that it is becoming increasingly difficult to sort out fiction from fact, and serious observation from hoax. Bigfoot is Big Business;[1] it attracts tourists, sells newspapers, books, souvenirs and plane rides over likely spotting points.

Literally thousands of Sasquatch stories may be found in the pages of the extensive Bigfoot literature, discussed, compared, analyzed and criticized exhaustively by those who make it their business to do so, but it is worth considering some of the early accounts before Sasquatch became big news. As long ago as 1784 the London *Times* reported that a 'huge, manlike, hair-covered' creature had been captured by Indians at a place called Lake of the Woods in Manitoba. Exactly a hundred years later the *Colonist*, the local paper of Victoria, British Columbia, published the following extraordinary story in its 4 July edition, under the headline, 'What is it? A strange creature captured above Yale. A British Columbian Gorilla':

In the immediate vicinity of No. 4 tunnel, situated some twenty miles above this village [Yale], are bluffs of rock which have hitherto been insurmountable, but on Monday morning last were successfully scaled by Mr. Onderson's employes [sic] on the regular train from Lytton. Mr. Costerton, the British Columbia Express Company's messenger, and a number of men from Lytton and points east of that place . . . succeeded in capturing a creature which may truly be called half man and half beast. 'Jacko', as the creature has been called by his capturers, is something of the gorilla type standing about four feet seven inches in height and weighing 127 pounds. He has long, black, strong hair and resembles a human being with one exception, his entire body, excepting his hands (or paws) and feet is covered with glossy hair about one inch long. His forearm is much longer than a man's forearm, and he possesses extraordinary strength, as he will take hold of a stick and break it by wrenching it or twisting it, which no man living could break in the same way. Since his capture he is very reticent, only occasionally uttering a noise which is half bark and half growl. He is, however, becoming daily more attached to his keeper, Mr. George Tilbury, of this place, who proposes shortly starting for London, England, to exhibit him. His favourite food so far is berries, and he drinks fresh milk with evident relish. By advice of Dr. Hannington raw meats have been withheld from Jacko, as the doctor thinks it would have a tendency to make him a savage. The mode of capture was as follows: Ned Austin, the engineer, on coming in sight of the bluff at the eastern end of the No. 4 tunnel saw what he supposed to be a man lying asleep in close proximity to the track, and as quick as thought blew the signal to apply the brakes. The brakes were instantly applied, and in a few seconds the train was brought to a standstill. At this moment the supposed man sprang up and, uttering a sharp quick bark, began to climb the steep bluff. Conductor R.J. Craig and express messenger Costerton, followed by the baggageman and brakesmen, jumped from the train, and knowing they were some twenty minutes ahead of time immediately gave chase. After five minutes of perilous climbing the then supposed demented Indian was corralled on a projecting shelf of rock where he could neither ascend nor descend. The query now was how to capture him alive, which was quickly decided by Mr. Craig, who crawled on his hands and knees until he was about forty feet above the creature. Taking a small piece of loose rock he let it fall and it had the desired effect of rendering poor Jacko incapable of resistance for a time at least. The bell rope was then brought up and Jacko was now lowered to terra firma. After firmly binding him and placing him in the baggage car, 'off brakes' was sounded and the train started for Yale. At the station a large crowd who had heard of the capture by telephone from Spuzzum Flat were assembled, each one anxious to have the first look at the monstrosity, but they were disappointed, as Jacko had been taken off at the machine shops and placed in charge of his present keeper.

The question naturally arises, how came the creature where it was first seen by Mr. Austin? From bruises about its head and body, and apparent soreness since its capture, it is supposed that Jacko ventured too near the edge of the bluff, slipped, fell, and lay where found until the sound of the rushing train aroused him. Mr. Thos. White and Mr. Gouin, C.E., as well as Mr. Major, who kept a small store about half a mile west of the tunnel during the past two years, have mentioned having seen a curious creature at different points between Camps 13 and 17, but no attention was paid to their remarks as people came to the conclusion that they had seen either a bear or a stray Indian dog. Who can unravel the mystery that now surrounds Jacko? Does he belong to a species hitherto unknown in this part of the continent, or is he really what the train men first thought he was, a crazy Indian?

The newspaper account of Jacko was subsequently confirmed by an old man, August Castle, who was a child in the town at the time. The fate of the captive is not known, although some said that he (accompanied by Mr Tilbury) was shipped east by rail in a cage on the way to be exhibited in a sideshow, but died in transit. The same paper recorded a consistent stream of other sightings from then on.

One of the best of the recent Sasquatch review articles comes from an 'old hand', John Green,[2] who undertook a study of more than a thousand reported sightings, working on the principle that *if* such a creature exists then a substantial proportion of the reports are likely to involve genuine observations of it – and if these are consistent, a portrait may emerge. Two of the stories are especially interesting since they have been the subject of sworn testimonies, although both were recorded some years after they happened. The so-called Chapman story came from a simple American Indian family living in Ruby Creek on the Frazer River, British Columbia. The farm was visited one day in 1940 by an 8-ft high male Sasquatch which emerged from the woods and approached the farmstead. Mrs Chapman grabbed the children and fled, having looked carefully at the creature (which she had thought at first was a bear – an animal with which she was familiar). When all was clear the family returned to the house to find it encircled by large footprints, 16 in. long and 8 in. wide, giving a pace length of 4 ft. A heavy barrel of salted fish had also been overturned and the contents scattered. The descriptions and dimensions of the creature are well within known Sasquatch limits for males, and the incident (notably the Sasquatch predilection for fish) is not without its parallels in Russian sightings (Pamirs).

A slightly later and even more famous sighting took place in 1955 when William Roe, a road builder and experienced hunter and woodsman, was exploring an area of the Mica Mountains in British Columbia. He saw a female Sasquatch, some 6 ft 3 in. tall and very broad, fully covered in dark brown silver-tipped hair and with heavy breasts. Roe noted long arms and broad feet, and that when the creature walked it put its heels down first, a characteristic of human walking or striding. The head seemed higher at the back than the front, the nose was flat, the creature had manlike ears and small dark eyes. He particularly noted the very short, almost non-existent neck, but was not given long to complete his observations because the Sasquatch walked rapidly away, watching him over its shoulder as it went.

One must also quote the famous account of Albert Ostman, a lumberman of Scandinavian origin who claimed he was captured by a Sasquatch while on a hunting and camping vacation in the area at the head of Toba inlet, opposite Vancouver Island, in 1924. Ostman did not tell his strange story for many years, on the reasonable grounds that he thought it might not be believed. He estimated that the Sasquatch, which had picked him up one night still in his sleeping bag, had carried him some 25 miles over the mountains. He found himself in the presence of a complete family: father, mother, son and younger daughter in a cliff-enclosed valley, where he remained for six days without being menaced. He provided very clear descriptions of the family, from whom he eventually escaped, stressing their humanlike behaviour although they had neither fire nor tools. Were it not for a sworn statement thirty-three years later in front of a Justice of the Peace at Fort Langley, British Columbia, and favourable reports from other investigators, one would have no difficulty in dismissing the story as a dream or a fantasy or (more unkindly) a publicity stunt for cash. Yet it did happen long before the publicity boom, and there are other accounts of people being captured by wildmen.

Various aspects of Ostman's story do not, however, ring true, including certain features of his descriptions which fail to match the extensive volume of reports now collected. For example, he mentioned that the creatures ate roots, tubers and tree-shoots, although they did not devote much of their time and energy to getting food. This seems unlikely, because large vegetarian primates spend virtually their whole waking existence gathering food, and the nutritional value of the fruits, berries and shoots in these coniferous forest areas is very low, making sheer quantity even more important. Thus the story is suspect. Most evidence points to the Sasquatch being an omnivore – an animal opportunist which eats anything suitable that happens to be around.

A typical recent sighting took place at 8 a.m. on 6 June 1978, when two men, Kendall and Hathaway, both in their fifties and senior survey engineers with a long experience of outdoor work, had just left their pick-up truck and were walking quietly along a high ridge in the northern Cascade Mountains in Washington State at an altitude of about 4,000 ft. It was a fine morning, the air crisp and cold, and thoughts of Bigfoot (of which neither of them had seen so much as a footprint, despite all their years in the heart of his country) were far from their minds. Suddenly the attention of both men was drawn to a large dark figure which moved quickly out of the broken scrub of an old logging operation directly opposite them. At first they thought it was just a man, and then they remembered that there was no logging in the area and that they were on a private, contracted timber reserve. They took another look and saw that the figure was very large, manlike and upright-walking, and striding purposefully towards cover in the form of a patch of dense timber. The creature was dark brown and totally covered with hair. They could see a head, arms and massive shoulders just for a second or two before it disappeared. Apparently they looked at each other, speechless with amazement, and began to walk to where it had disappeared to look for footprints, but the ground was hard and stony and they could find nothing. Both men are now convinced that what they saw was a Sasquatch, although previously they would have said it was impossible for such a creature to survive unknown in an area which they knew so well.[3]

Kendall and Hathaway are not the only sceptics who allowed themselves to be convinced by the evidence of their own eyes. In 1958 Jerry Crew, a tough 'catskinner' (the man who bulldozes logging roads), came upon manlike tracks in the mud which measured 16 in. long and 7 in. wide and seemed to be in places which would defy the ingenuity of even the most cunning of hoaxers with a footprint machine. Mr Crew and his team had observed these and similar tracks for several weeks, and on this occasion he was moved to make a plaster cast of the prints. The publication of his finds, and the fact that the tracks had been found by people who were not looking for them, produced a veritable flood of reports of previous sightings and tracks, some of which could have been true. The Crew prints were especially interesting since they were found near Bluff Creek Valley which, together with the Onion Mountain and Blue Creek Mountain, forms a region of 40 sq. miles covered with dense coniferous forests and seems to be a Sasquatch homeland. Since vast tracts of similar countryside in the Pacific Northwest are almost completely unexplored, it is not altogether unlikely that the Sasquatch might survive there.

On the night of 21 October 1972, Alan Berry, a journalist living in Sacramento, California, recorded the voice of Bigfoot, at an altitude of about 8,500 ft in the High Sierras of northern California, some 2,000 ft above the nearest road and 8 miles from the nearest trail. Members of his group made previous and subsequent recordings at the same location, but this one is of exceptionally high quality. It has a wide range of sounds, some of which seem quite humanlike, and even some whistles. Subsequent work on the tapes involved techniques of signal processing, and the range of the recorded pitch and vocal length indicated a creature whose vocal tract was much larger than man's. The tape was not pre-recorded, nor had it been tampered with in any way, obviating the possibility

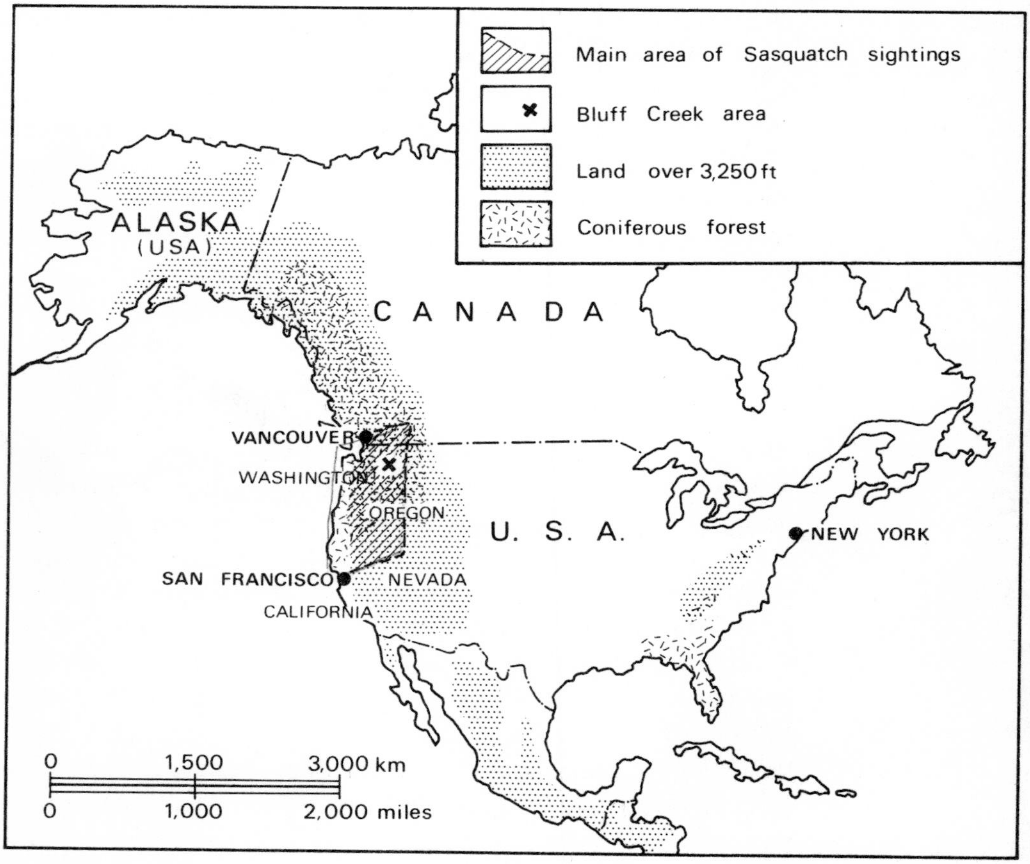

Main area of Sasquatch sightings

Bluff Creek area

Land over 3,250 ft

Coniferous forest

ALASKA
(USA)

CANADA

VANCOUVER
WASHINGTON
OREGON
U.S.A.
NEW YORK
SAN FRANCISCO
NEVADA
CALIFORNIA

| 0 | 1,500 | 3,000 km |
| 0 | 1,000 | 2,000 miles |

*9 Sightings of Sasquatch (Bigfoot) in North America.*

of a hoax. Data from an 'average' man (5 ft 11 in. high, 7-in. long vocal tract and average pitch of 115 Hz) suggested that the creature on the recording had a proportional height of up to 8 ft 4 in., but slightly different results were obtained depending on which sound was analyzed. (The 'grr' growl sound, for example, yielded a height for the creature of between 7 ft 4 in. and 8 ft 2 in.). Serious analysis of the sounds having precluded hoaxing, one is left with the conclusion that the tape was genuine, and moreover, that more than one Bigfoot seems to have been heard.[4]

'Soft' evidence for the existence of Sasquatch includes faeces and hair, but again there remains a certain measure of doubt about their origins. In one study of five preserved faeces and three specimens of hair, two of the former and two of the latter were definitely attributable to known animals but the others were not.[5] Faecal attribution is carried out on the basis of shape and contents and involves rehydrating the mass and identifying its constituents. A great deal of work has been done on both animal and human faeces, especially in archaeological contexts, with the object of reconstructing ancient patterns of diet and disease.[6] In the case of the Sasquatch we have relatively little information about its diet, although most people seem to be in broad agreement that it is an omnivore. There are really only thirteen reliable reports of Sasquatch eating habits, of which nine refer to vegetable foods and only four to the eating of meat. It would seem reasonable to suggest that the Sasquatch has a preference for vegetation, but will consume lesser quantities of almost anything else that comes its way – items such as tree roots, grass, berries and deer meat figure prominently on the menu. One list of foods apparently occasionally eaten in lesser quantities includes bears, sheep, chickens, cows, horses, rodents and other small animals, grubs, clams, fish including salmon, eggs and bacon, milk and doughnuts!

There have been various attempts at identifying hair samples purported to come from a Sasquatch. Some samples can be attributed to known animals, but there are others which do not match those from any known animal species and have both human and non-human characteristics. To date, no one has found a single hair which can be *definitely* attributed to a Sasquatch, but some of the specimens thought to have come from them are extremely puzzling.

The most controversial and at the same time potentially convincing evidence for the Sasquatch so far is the film shot on 20 October 1967 by Roger Patterson when trekking on horseback high up in the Bluff Creek Valley of northern California, an area where many footprints had already been found. Patterson himself had followed the Sasquatch saga for several years and even published a flamboyant journalistic paperback called *Do Abominable Snowmen of America really exist?*[7] For this reason alone critics dismissed his film as a hoax, or at least a fraud designed to cash in on the subject.

Patterson and his partner Bob Gimlin were crossing rough country along the base of a bluff when they rounded a sharp bend in a creek and the horses reared, throwing both men. The cause of the alarm was a large animal which they could see across the creek about 90 ft away, conforming closely to known descriptions of the Sasquatch. Patterson grabbed his movie camera (fortunately already loaded) and started running towards the creature, filming as he went. Since he was running, the resulting film is jerky and the image rather blurred, and in his haste he forgot to note the film speed, two facts which inflamed the subsequent controversy. The result, however, is a continuous sequence of 20 ft of colour film which seems to show a female Sasquatch, about 7 ft high and weighing an estimated 350 pounds. Her pendulous breasts are clearly visible, and she is covered with short shiny black hair, with the exception of the area just around her eyes. On the back of her head there is a kind of ridge (a bony crest observed on other Sasquatch, which also occurs, incidentally, on large female gorillas), and she has a very short neck, heavy back and shoulder muscles. The creature walked upright, swinging its arms, in a humanlike manner. Patterson, running as fast as he could after the creature and trying to focus the camera at the same time, was surprised when she turned to face him and did not seem at all frightened by his proximity. Of course, she was much the larger animal. However, this enabled him to get a head-and-shoulders shot before she ambled off into the forest.

Gimlin, meanwhile, had been trying to control the horses, which seemed to have been frightened either by the appearance of the creature or by its foul smell – the latter being a feature remarked by both men at the time, and one which has been noted in association with other sightings (and of the Yeti). The two men followed the creature's tracks (she had moved with a pace of 40–42 in.) until they were cut off by a tributary stream. They then headed back for the nearest town to get the film processed and to summon some scientific help.[8] Rene Dahinden, an acknowledged Sasquatch expert, arrived at Bluff Creek the day after filming, but it had rained heavily in the night and the creek had risen quickly. Although they managed to make a cast of one of the prints the danger of flooding forced them to leave the area. Further corroborative evidence being denied them the burden of proof rested on the film alone, which generated a vast amount of public interest when news of its existence was released. It has since been shown on many occasions in the USA, in Russia, Britain, Europe, on television, at conferences, and to interested scientists. There is still no firm consensus. Everything hangs on one question – would it be possible for the figure to be that of a hoaxer, an actor in a fur suit, and could such a deception be carried out sufficiently well to fool the scientific establishment?

In order to solve the problem, a detailed analysis of the creature's movements and characteristics is required, but this is complicated by the fact that the frame speed of the film is unknown. Patterson's camera was equipped to run at 16 or 24 frames per second (fps), and he cannot remember which setting he used. The question is crucial, for if the sequence had been filmed at 24 fps the creature's walk could not be distinguished from that of a normal human being, but at 16 fps there are a number of features which are definitely not human. Gimlin showed the film to the special effects technicians who had created King Kong and asked whether, in their opinion, they could reproduce the figure. Their answer was interesting: 'We could try, but we would have to create a completely new system of artificial muscles and find an actor who could be trained to walk like that. It might be done, but we would have to say that it would be almost impossible.'[9] This seems to agree with the majority view that the film could be a hoax, but if so an incredibly clever one.

Don Grieve, Reader in Biomechanics at the Royal Free Hospital, London, said that if the film had been shot at the faster speed the model could have been an actor, but Grieve could see the muscle masses in the right places and that would be most difficult to fake. The terrific breadth of the shoulders, so characteristic of Sasquatch, would be difficult to imitate, since the padding necessary to achieve that effect would result in unnatural contours and very stilted swinging of the arms. There is a slight disagreement about the height of the creature in the film – some say about 7 ft and some rather less, around 6 ft 5 in. – and one means of testing the possibility of a hoax is to examine the relationship between height and size of footprints, whose casts in this case are $14\frac{1}{2}$ in. long. There appears to be a very good correlation between an estimated height of 6 ft 5 in., a calculated step length for that height of 41 in. and Patterson's actual ground measurement of 42 in., making it quite a small Sasquatch and well within the maximum height range of males of our own species. The skin *could* be faked by a fur suit over a polystyrene foam 'musculature', but this would surely be detectable. In conclusion one can only repeat that, if it is a hoax, it is brilliant. If not, then it is the first film ever taken of an unclassified species of great ape.

The review article published by John Green in *Manlike Monsters on Trial* (1980) provides perhaps the best summary of the current state of our knowledge about the Sasquatch. Green concludes that the popular idea of Bigfoot as a rare hominid is incorrect; it seems to be an inoffensive large bipedal ape with a secure population and widespread distribution. In addition to the thousand or so reports analyzed by Green, many more exist, mostly describing footprints markedly similar in size and shape. Green's study produced the following 'identikit' Sasquatch:

*Height* 74 per cent reported larger than man, with average height calculated at 7 ft 6 in. except in Oregon, where the average exceeds 8 ft. All Sasquatch are consistently taller than humans of comparable age and sex. They are also built quite differently, 'heavy' or 'very heavy' in build and much wider than the average human.

*Habits* Most observations are of solitary creatures. Reports specifically identifying females and young are very rare. Only 5 per cent involve more than one individual, and only 1 per cent more than two. Sasquatch are observed to be largely nocturnal, which is in itself interesting since there are fewer human observers around at night than during the day, and we do not have good night vision. Fifty per cent of all sightings are reported at night, and one estimate says that almost 90 per cent of tracks were also made at night.

*Appearance* Broad shoulders, short necks, flat faces, large flat noses, sloping foreheads and brow ridges combined with great height and heavy build to give a 'primitive' appearance. Sasquatch are uniformly furry, rather than hairy, and less than 8 per cent of observers said that the hair was longer on the head than the body (as it is in man), rather than about the same length all over (as in a gorilla).

Sasquatch seem to be omnivorous, and there is a marked seasonal variation in observations suggesting that they might hibernate. Everywhere except Florida has only half as many reports in winter (as opposed to summer or autumn) and tracks in snow are rare, as are spring sightings. The connection between these primates and water is very strong, just as it is in the case of the Siberian Yeti-like creature. Six reports tell of tracks ending in lakes or rivers, five of Sasquatch swimming, and twelve of them standing or walking in water. A large proportion of the tracks are beside water. Other interesting behaviour patterns emerge, with varying degrees of substantiation. There are a few examples of Sasquatch throwing things at people (without hitting them), chasing them (without catching them), looking in house or car windows or, very rarely, grabbing people (seven accounts). The details of face and feature vary slightly, as do descriptions of gait and movement, but sounds seem to be quite rare except for a kind of scream, and there are no accounts of tool-making or fire-using, nor do the creatures often use their hands to carry food. The general picture is of a large, inoffensive ape.

In many ways the Sasquatch has perhaps diverged from its ape ancestors, and its behaviour is certainly very different from that of probably its nearest living relative, the mountain gorilla. It can swim, see in the dark, survive in a wide variety of climates, and does not require complex social organization and hierarchies (like the gorilla, chimpanzee or baboon). Its only resemblance to a human being is that it is bipedal – it walks upright – but in all other respects it is very different. However, like man it is not an endangered species, since the unfrequented hundreds of thousands of square miles of suitable habitat in the mountains of the Pacific Northwest seem to support a large population. No estimate can definitively be reached, but Green suggested that it might be useful to consider the grizzly bear as a parallel. Grizzlies require large territories and are found over a much smaller area than Sasquatch, yet their numbers are always estimated in multiples of ten thousand. The Sasquatch population must number at least in the thousands, and possibly many thousands. Since all efforts to hunt one have failed, it is clear that the Sasquatch has a strong sense of self-preservation and, indeed, may even be adept at hiding its tracks or evading dogs.

There is a striking degree of internal consistency in reports of Sasquatch sightings and footprints. Extensive studies of the latter have now been carried out by eminent anatomists which generally agree with Napier, who wrote in 1972:[10]

One might pose the question: who other than God or natural selection is sufficiently conversant with the subtleties of the human foot and the human walking style to 'design' an artificial foot which is so perfectly harmonious in terms of structure and function?

Easily the most impressive of the tracks comes from Bossburg, near the Canadian border in Washington State, where a series of 1,089 prints were found from a crippled Sasquatch whose right foot was a clubfoot (*Talipes-equino-varus*), most likely the result of a crushing injury in childhood, and quite unfakeable. The average length of normal tracks varies gradually in a south-north direction from 15 in. in California to $18\frac{1}{2}$ in. in Canada, correlating with a gradual increase in average stature (7 ft 4 in. in California and 8 ft 8 in. in Western Canada). Statistical tests suggest that these variations are genuine and not the result of sampling bias, but of course this proves only that the size variations are real and apparently regulated from south to north – it does not say that their maker is real, even if this might be a legitimate inference.[11] The south-north increase in body size is especially interesting since it conforms to a well-known ecological principle, Bergmann's Rule, which states that populations of a species which live nearer the poles tend to have a larger body size than those at the equator. Bigger bodies have smaller surface areas per volume than smaller ones, and can thus conserve heat better in cooler temperatures.[12] Other species which live in the general area of Sasquatch distribution also conform to this rule – as does man himself.[13]

In Sasquatch there also appears to be a south-north variation in coat colour (although nearly 14 per cent of California and Oregon Sasquatch are beige or white, the vast majority are brown or black), but in Washington State and Western Canada 26 per cent have light coats. These trends of body height, footprint length and coat colour all conform to general biogeographical principles and support statistical investigations, within a geographical span of over a thousand miles and nearly a hundred years of observations.

In the light of the sheer wealth of reasonably reliable information that is now being gathered, there is a gradual change in scientists' attitudes, and something of a 'no smoke without fire' approach is emerging. Bigfoot studies are attracting research grants, research centres are being established and results are being published in reputable academic journals. Learned societies approve Bigfoot studies, and universities sponsor conferences.

The Bigfoot Information Center at Hood River, Oregon, has a small staff who steadily examine, analyze and compile what they term 'supportive evidence' from the steady stream of information provided by the public. Some 98 per cent of this material is disregarded as worthless, and the rest falls into three categories: history, footprints and sightings. Since the establishment of the Center its staff have interviewed 300 people who have claimed sightings, but only 96 of these have been entered as genuine, the best and most credible certainly being that of Kendall and Hathaway, which inspired a well-researched, serious documentary film *Manbeast* made for American television. The Center also publishes *Bigfoot News* with a circulation of 10,000, dealing not only with 'homegrown' hominids but with foreign news as well. Its active monitoring of Bigfootiana and the involvement of foreign correspondents (notably dealing with Russian sources – the tireless Bayanov and Burtsev from the Darwin Museum, Moscow) make it easily the most up-to-date source of useful information for enthusiasts.

Indeed the Sasquatch is now respectable, and it is thought to be narrow-minded not to believe in its existence. As long ago as 1969 the following proclamation appeared in Skamania County, Oregon, heartland of Sasquatchery:

ORDINANCE No. 69–01.

Be it hereby ordained by the Board of County Commissioners of Skamania County:

WHEREAS, there is evidence to indicate the possible existence in Skamania County of a nocturnal primate mammal variously described as an ape-like creature or a sub-species of Homo Sapiens, and

WHEREAS, both legend and purported recent sightings and spoor support this possibility, and

WHEREAS, this creature is generally and commonly known as a 'Sasquatch', 'Yeti', 'Bigfoot', or 'Giant Hairy Ape', and

WHEREAS, publicity attendant upon such real or imagined sightings has resulted in an influx of scientific investigators as well as casual hunters, many armed with lethal weapons, and

WHEREAS, the absence of specific laws covering the taking of specimens encourages laxity in the use of fire-arms and other deadly devices and poses a clear and present threat to the safety and well-being of persons living or travelling within the boundaries of Skamania County as well as to the creatures themselves,

THEREFORE BE IT RESOLVED that any premeditated, wilful and wanton slaying of any such creature shall be deemed a felony punishable by a fine not to exceed Ten Thousand Dollars ($10,000.00) and/or imprisonment in the county jail for a period not to exceed Five (5) years.

BE IT FURTHER RESOLVED that the situation existing constitutes an emergency and as such this ordinance is effective immediately.

ADOPTED this 1st day of April 1969.
    Board of Commissioners of Skamania County.
    By: Conrad Lundy Jr., Chairman.
    Approved:    Robert K. Leick, Skamania County
                  Prosecuting Attorney.

The anomaly appears to be that one can be sent to jail by the authorities for shooting something that they do not officially admit exists. Of all the Sasquatch paradoxes, this must surely be the most splendid.

The nature of the footprints and many of the descriptions of the Sasquatch and the Chinese Yeti (Chapter 4) tally quite closely. Assuming they both exist, they could be closely related through descent from the supposedly extinct great ape *Gigantopithecus*, which seems to have lived in the right area at the right time to serve as a common ancestor. The distance between America and Asia is not great – a mere 52 miles of Bering Strait (with very similar patterns of land on each side) which has at different periods in the past, when sea level was lower, been joined by a land bridge.

North America has no other primates today, but this has not always been the case. A single upper molar tooth was sifted from tons of rubble at a site in Montana called Purgatory Hill, and must represent a primate which, with its friends, was living in North America at least 40 million years ago when the link with Eurasia probably broke as a part of gradual drifting and formation of continents.[14] In Europe and Asia the primate ancestors seem to have migrated southwards and there started to evolve. The only New World primates are the monkeys, found in Central and South America, which have evolved in a manner very reminiscent of their Old World monkey relatives through being subjected to separate but similar environmental pressures. But there were no North American primates to evolve into the Sasquatch, so it would have evolved somewhere else and migrated to North America. In order to suggest when this could have happened it is necessary to consider the geological evidence. We know that *Gigantopithecus* had evolved in Asia at least 9 million years ago, and was still going strong 8 million years later. If therefore at any time during that period there was a land bridge between Siberia and North America, it would have been possible for the creatures to cross.

If the Sasquatch is a gigantopithecine then it is likely to have reached America *before* the beginning of the Ice Age around 1.8 million years ago – at a time when we know *Gigantopithecus* was flourishing in China. The many sea-level fluctuations of the Ice Age included only two late periods when the land bridge connecting Siberia and Alaska was open, between 36,000 and 32,000 years ago, and 28,000 and 13,000 years ago. The first *Home sapiens sapiens* bands seem to have crossed during the first period and the early part of the second, using a convenient glacier-free corridor into the heart of North America which was closed about 20,000 years ago at the period of maximum glacial expansion. If the Sasquatch had also crossed at this late date – and one assumes it is related to the primates of Asia – then one would expect it to resemble the Yeti more than it seems on present evidence to do.

It is rather agreeable to think (in these days of perilous global politics) of Chinese gigantopithecines ambling calmly across the Bering Strait into the American Continent. And of course there is no reason why they should not have done so, taking advantage of new resources offered by similar terrain. This is not to suggest that both American and Chinese varieties have not evolved considerably *in situ* since that time; but it does make sound geographical and zoological sense to suggest that their ultimate origins probably lie in the same population and general area.

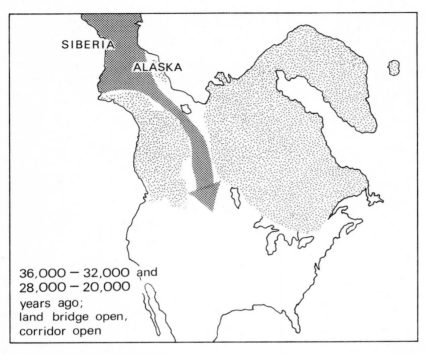

SIBERIA
ALASKA

36,000 – 32,000 and
28,000 – 20,000
years ago;
land bridge open,
corridor open

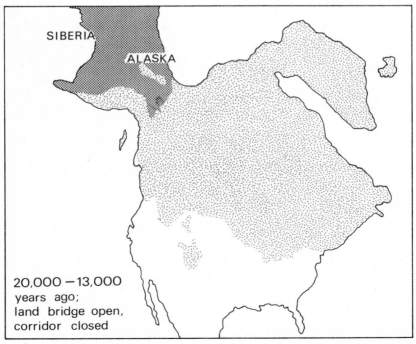

SIBERIA
ALASKA

20,000 – 13,000
years ago;
land bridge open,
corridor closed

10 *Man probably first crossed from Asia into the heartland of North America some 36,000-20,000 years ago, when Ice Age glaciers locked up the waters of the Bering Sea – thus creating a land bridge between Siberia and Alaska – but were not so extensive that they blocked passage south through Canada. The Sasquatch could also have crossed at this late date, but other evidence suggests an earlier arrival, before the beginning of the Ice Age 1.8 million years ago.*

## Chapter 3
# The Original
# Yeti

Almost everything about the Yeti is controversial, even the name. Tracks, sightings, scalps, mummified hands, folk legends and oral tradition are all interpreted in different ways by different people, resulting in the accumulation of an extensive literature. But is the Yeti just a legend, or can we find scientific proof of its existence and nature? Perhaps we should not even be calling it a Yeti (the name I have selected here as being reasonably uncontentious), since the Nepalese recognize two different sorts of Snowman (*yeh-teh*), *dzu-teh* and *meh-teh*. The *dzu-teh* is, however, generally accepted to be a large, hairy, red bear which is aggressive and hunts cattle, and when the Sherpas of Nepal speak of the *yeh-teh* (*yeti* in its Anglicized form), they mean the smaller ape – or manlike *meh-teh*, not *dzu-teh*. The extraordinary name 'Abominable Snowman' seems to have been invented in 1930 by one Henry Newman, a journalist in Calcutta, derived from the Tibetan *meteh kang-mi* (according to H.W. Tilman), meaning 'filthy or disgusting man-of-the-snows'; but this origin is much disputed and *meteh* is in any case more correctly spelt *metoh*. Other names include *mirka*, *mi-go*, *sogpa* or *shukpa* (in Sikkim).

The worldwide fame of the Yeti is largely due to the activities of mountaineers this century who have publicized its existence. But Yetis were already being recorded by the British military and Indian Civil Service during the 19th century. B.H. Hodgson, British Resident at the Nepalese court from 1820 to 1843, is generally credited with the first mention of the Yeti in Western literature, when he noted that some of his porters had been frightened by a hairy, tailless wildman in northern Nepal. In 1889 Major L.A. Waddell found the first large footprints in snow at 17,000 ft in Sikkim, and was told by *his* porters that he was looking at Yeti tracks. With hearty British scepticism he dismissed them as those of the snow bear, *Ursus isabellinus*. A whole period of 'amateur' sightings followed before the advent of serious climbing expeditions in the 1930s, when the Everest area became the focus of interest for a large number of Westerners. The very first Everest reconnaissance expedition under Lieutenant-Colonel C.K. Howard-Bury in 1921 saw human-like footprints on Llakpa-La between 20,000 and 21,000 ft, and there was a report of an actual sighting by N.A. Tonbazi in 1925, who saw a Yeti on the Zemu glacier at 15,000 ft. These events started an extensive correspondence from interested parties. A glance at page 11 of *The Times* for Thursday, 3 November 1921, will show Howard-Bury's dispatch from Everest, but the same page also contains the following:

## "ABOMINABLE SNOWMEN"

### A TRAVELLER'S EXPERIENCE

TO THE EDITOR OF THE TIMES.

Sir,

Dr. Douglas Freshfield has had better opportunities than most men of confirming or explaining the belief current in Sikkim, among the people of the higher valleys, that "wild men" exist.

I can hardly believe that the tracks in the snow seen by some members of the Everest Expedition would have been mentioned in a telegram if there were any question that the tracks were those of a human being.

When I was travelling in the forests on the Nepal frontier of British Sikkim in March 1914, with Mr. Gent, then Forest Officer of the Darjeeling district, he told me that the coolies employed by him in cutting jungle at an elevation of 8,000–9,000 ft. had been on more than one occasion driven from their work by what they believed to be wild men. I was unable to cross-examine the men who reported this, but I asked Mr. Gent to make further enquiries, and he, being a good shikari, would have known the tracks of a bear from those of a human being. I thought it possible that the tracks of a large langur monkey, which goes up to 9,000–10,000 ft. in Sikkim, might have been mistaken for human tracks.

But the war put an end to this, as to many other scientific enquiries, and we must await the return of the expedition for more definite information as to what they actually saw.

The Athenaeum, Nov. 2.                                   H.J. ELWES

Mr. William Hugh Knight, a member of the Royal Societies Club, recalled yesterday to a representative of The Times an occasion some years ago when he was able to inspect closely a figure which he believes to be that of one of the "Abominable Snowmen" to whom reference has been made by members of the Everest Expedition. He said:

'Shortly before the last Tibetan War I was returning from Tibet with another European, a Tibetan guide, and our train of about 40 or 50 coolies. We were coming down the track that leads from Gantok to Sedonchen. We wanted to go to Gantok by the higher track but Tenzin Wagdi, our guide, said the coolies would not face the leeches, so we had to take the lower track, which roughly follows the river. As we got near Gantok we had to climb the long ascent. My companion had gone on ahead with the coolies. I was about half a mile behind, about half a mile below Gantok.

I stopped to breathe my horse on an open clearing and dismounted, loosened the girths, and watched the sun, which was just about setting. While I was musing I heard a slight sound, and looking round, I saw, some 15 or 20 paces away, a figure which I now suppose must have been one of the hairy men that the Everest Expedition talk about and the Tibetans, according to them, call the "Abominable Snowmen".

Speaking to the best of my recollection, he was a little under 6 ft. high, almost stark naked in that bitter cold – it was the month of November. He was a kind of pale yellow all over, about the colour of a Chinaman, a shock of matted hair on his head, little hair on his face, highly splayed feet, and large, formidable hands. His muscular development in the arms, thighs, legs, back and chest were terrific. He had in his hand what seemed to me to be some form of primitive bow. He did not see me, but stood there, and I watched for some five or six minutes. So far as I could make out, he was watching some man or beast far down the hillside. At the end of some five minutes he started off at a run down the hill, and I was impressed with the tremendous speed at which he travelled.

So far as I can remember, I mentioned the matter in the Gurkha mess that night, and to Claude White when I saw him at the Residence the next morning, but my recollection is that they took it rather as a matter of course. The incident more or less passed out of my mind until I read about the tracks in the snow written of by members of the Everest Expedition.'

With one exception, the European sightings that followed came either from mountaineering expeditions (which are more likely to find the footprints than their makers) or from deliberately mounted Yeti-hunting ventures. The said exception is the most detailed description of a Snowman yet, and comes from a story told by Slavomir Rawicz who, with six friends, escaped from a Siberian prisoner-of-war camp and travelled across the Himalayas to India.

The sighting is supposed to have taken place somewhere between Bhutan and Sikkim in February 1942, but is not precisely located. The men saw two black specks moving across the snow about a quarter of a mile below them when descending a mountain. From slightly closer to the creatures seemed 'enormous and they walked on their hind legs'. Rawicz says that he and his companions were incredulous but frightened that the creatures might attack them, which prevented them from trying to get any nearer. He estimated their height at not much less than 8 ft, noting that one was a few inches taller than the other in the same relation as a man's height is to a woman's. The heads were described as 'squarish and the ears must lie close to the skull because there was no projection from the silhouette against the snow. The shoulders sloped sharply down to a powerful chest. The arms were long and the wrists reached the level of the knees. Seen in profile the back of the head was a straight line from the crown into the shoulders, described by one of the party as 'like a damned Prussian'. Both creatures were covered by reddish brown hair which formed a close body fur mixed with long straight hairs hanging downwards. Rawicz's party continued to observe the creatures (which showed no reciprocal interest) for about an hour before trying to chase them away with shouting and snowballs, but when this failed and the creatures showed no fear the men gave up and decided to take a detour.[1]

It is most unfortunate that all this detail occurs in a book whose authenticity is, to say the least, doubtful. Various geographers and alpinists have pointed out numerous inconsistencies in the route which Rawicz claimed he and his companions took, in particular Eric Shipton (finder of the first and best footprint trail), who noted among other things that the route described should have included the crossing of a busy main highway and that there are discrepancies of date — one stretch of the journey which apparently took Rawicz two months, should, so Shipton calculated using Rawicz's own estimate of his speed, have taken only five days.[2]

From the 1930s onwards, footprints were seen by expedition personnel, including such notable figures as John (now Lord) Hunt (leader of the British Expedition to Mt Everest in 1953), Eric Shipton, H. W. Tilman, and Sir Edmund Hillary (conqueror of Everest with Sherpa Tenzing in May 1953). Indeed, even the doubters admit that Shipton's famous footprints, seen on the Menlung Glacier in 1951, cannot readily be explained away. Together with Michael Ward, Shipton was returning in November 1951 from an Everest reconnaissance expedition. They were exploring the saddle at the head of the Menlung Glacier close to the Nepal/Tibet border near 18,000 ft when they came across a set of tracks in deep snow and followed them for about a mile along the edge of the glacier. Although the famous, often-reproduced single footprint was not one from the trail, but taken earlier in the day in roughly the same area, it has mysteriously endowed the whole Yeti business with respectability as being something discovered by people with no hope of commercial gain or need for sensational publicity.

Lord Hunt himself has remained a vigorous champion of the Yeti, since he has twice heard the creature's strange high-pitched call and come upon tracks in 1953 and 1978. In both cases the tracks were in snow and at high altitude (15,000–20,000 ft), well above the habitat of the Himalayan black and red bears. The tracks seen by Lord Hunt in 1978 were very fresh, and it was possible to see the impression of toes, convincing him that the footprint represented the actual size and shape of the feet, about $13\frac{3}{4}$ in. long and $6\frac{3}{4}$ in. broad (a man with size 44 shoes has a print length of $11\frac{1}{2}$ in.). This is especially interesting since it has, of course, been frequently contended that such tracks are made either by other animals (bears or langurs being the most favoured), or by the impressions of human feet which have become exaggerated in the melting snow. Lord Hunt is on record, many years earlier, for having said in his foreword to Charles Stonor's book, *The Sherpa and the Snowman* (1955):

And I believe in the Yeti. I have seen his tracks, heard his yelping call, listened to first-hand experiences of reputable local people. . . . That evidence will be produced sooner or later, sufficient to convince the doubters, is beyond doubt.

Much more recently he expanded this statement as a result of a trip to Peking with a Parliamentary delegation (*Sunday Express*, 28 June 1981):

I talked to experts in Peking and discovered that the Chinese are doing a lot of research into this mystery. They showed me photographs of footprints found in China and Russia and they are remarkably similar to ones I have seen in the Himalayas. Now I'm even more convinced there is a very strong case in favour of the animal's existence. It is definitely not a bear. It looks more like an ape and the Chinese believe it could be a primitive form of man.

It has often been claimed that some of the footprints seen in the high snowfields of Tibet could have been made by *sadhus*, wandering Hindu holy men. Unclad ascetics, although relatively common in India, are rare in Tibet, but some do live in caves high up in the mountains. Their *tumo* training (the art of warming oneself up by the power of the mind) is said to enable them to survive the cruel winters at 11,000–18,000 ft. The *tumo* rites must be carried out in pure air far from habitation, so it is possible that these hermits might have left some tracks to be seen by mountaineers. But surely this cannot explain all the many Yeti tracks that have been reported over the years?[3]

In the 1950s the Yeti legend really took hold of the public imagination and 'folklore started to deteriorate into fakelore'.[4] During this period the Nepalese government, keen to cash in on the creature's tourist potential, issued Yeti-hunting licences at £400 per Yeti. The fact that none of the hunters was ever successful did not matter at all. But even during this intense commercialization tracks were still being seen by mountaineers, and in 1954 the famous *Daily Mail* expedition set off, its aim, to observe and if possible to capture a Yeti.[5] Despite the fact that the expedition took along firearms for protection, it had been decided on ethical grounds *not* to shoot a Yeti, but to resort to trapping, bribing the locals, attracting Yetis by means of bright objects or (failing that) by using nets, bolas, soporific drugs or hunting dogs. Stonor, a romantic at heart, described their dreams of capturing a specimen alive and photographing it in its own environment:

For my own part I rather favoured the possible quixotic ending to the story. The opened door of the cage; the Abominable Snowman taking a last look round his quarters and then shuffling off into the distance in imitation of the fade-out of a Charlie Chaplin film.[6]

In the event no Yetis were captured and the 'hunters' returned with nothing more than footprints and vague sightings. The expedition did, however, prompt an amusing verse in *Punch*:

## NOTHING DEFINITE YETI

There are fascinating footprints in the snows of Katmandu
On a slightly less than super-human scale:
There are numerous conjectures on the owner of the shoe
And the money it has cost the *Daily Mail.*

The *Daily Mail* fiasco was followed in 1957 by the first of three
huge expeditions financed by Texas oil millionaire Tom Slick,
which again returned with its quota of footprints, droppings and
hairs (the last two of dubious origin). The lack of success is not at all
surprising, because large, lavishly equipped expeditions are most
unlikely to see the Yeti. Noise and large numbers of people (300
porters at a time were employed by the *Daily Mail* team) are likely
to frighten away all the local fauna. There is nevertheless a clear
relationship between the number of people who visit an area and
the number of Snowmen reported there. This accounts for the
increase in Yeti sightings after mountaineering became fashionable
in the 1930s.

One further expedition, which explored the Arun Valley between
Everest and Kanchenjunga in 1972, is worth noting. Three Yeti
incidents were reported, including a nocturnal visit to one of the
expedition's tents by an animal 'which left tracks that are not
referable to any known animal'. The importance of this expedition
lies in its approach – not looking in the high snows but in the dense
Himalayan forested valleys, which may support the main Yeti
populations. This tropical montane forest is not unlike the habitat
of the mountain gorilla, and footprints produced do indeed show a
marked resemblance to those of a gorilla as well as a superficial
resemblance to Shipton's print, although they are much smaller ($8\frac{2}{3}$
in. long compared with 13 in.).

A curious, but in many ways typical, incident was reported by
Peter Matthiessen from northwest Nepal on the Tibetan frontier.
He had gone there with the twin objectives of accompanying his
friend, the zoologist George Schaller, in his studies of the
Himalayan blue sheep and snow leopard, and of making a personal
mystic pilgrimage to the region called Dolpo, whose religion and
culture have been little studied. Here is his account of the event,
recorded in his remarkable book, *The Snow Leopard* (1979):

Near a fork where a tributary stream flows down from the B'on village at Pung-mo, the deep forest across the torrent has been parted by an avalanche, and on this brushy slope a dark shape jumps behind a boulder. The slope is in bright morning sun, but I glimpse the creature only for an instant. It is much too big for a red panda, too covert for a musk deer, too dark for wolf or leopard, and much quicker than a bear. With binoculars, I stare for a long time at the mute boulder, feeling the presence of unknown life behind it, but all is still, there is only the sun and morning mountainside, the pouring water.

No animal that he had ever seen moved like this creature yet he was reluctant to think he might have had the luck to see a snowman. The area in question is a forested ravine comparable in altitude to the cloud forests of eastern Nepal like Arun Valley, where many snowmen have been sighted, but in this remote region unvisited by mountaineers or tourists, the creature was not thought to be common.

An even more intriguing sighting was made in Nepal by the mountaineers Don Whillans and Dougal Haston. One day in 1970, at 13,000 ft, they found and photographed a footprint trail which could have been made by a Yeti. That same night Whillans saw, at some distance from his tent but clear in the moonlight, an apelike creature 'bounding along on all fours'. Although the Sherpas often speak of the Yeti as being nocturnal, this is the first recorded European sighting at night.

So far we have heard the tales and sightings of Europeans, whose desire to believe in the Yeti has been almost as strong as the evidence produced is weak – or at least inconclusive. But what of native reports? Do they give clearer proof? Can we find firm evidence for the Yeti in the traditional culture and religion of Nepal and Tibet?

The Yeti was, it seems, well established as a part of Himalayan life and in the religion of Tibet long before it was brought to the attention of Westerners. The rituals of the ancient shamanistic B'on religion, precursor of Buddhist state lamaism, involved sacrifices needing the blood of a horse, dog, black bear, goat, pig, raven, man and wildman (Yeti). The rituals also required that the blood of the wildman should be obtained from a specimen killed by an arrow. In a ritual still followed at the Khumjung monastery a man dressed in a sheepskin and conical hat (representing a Yeti scalp) must appear, armed with a bow and arrow. The actor playing this hunter (not the most popular of roles) is considered to be cursed. The precise meaning of this symbolism is now unknown, but instructions for the ritual have been written down.

Tibetans see their universe overcrowded with supernatural beings, and make little distinction between the nature deities of the old folkways and the denizens of the Buddhist pantheon. The Yeti itself is a minor figure in Tibetan religious art, and may also be found in manuscripts, but it is very rare. At least one class of object, the cloth painting designed as a wall hanging and called *thankas* (or *thang-kas*), does seem to show the occasional Yeti or wildman.[7] Characteristically, they appear on paintings of the cosmos in a position above representations of the animal kingdom, but below the level of humanity.[8] They have white (hairless) knees and elbows, and often appear with a 'raised arm' posture.

Yetis also appear on *mandalas*, which show hierarchies of gods and demons with their attendants and are to be considered as aids to meditation. Here bears, apes and langurs are depicted clearly separate from the wildman, suggesting that there is no confusion (at least in the minds of the artists) between these forms. In the Tibetan zoological system man was thought to have evolved from the monkey, but the wildman was neither man nor monkey. Great confusion, unfortunately, exists in manuscripts because of difficulties in disentangling which words actually mean 'wildman', since one of the Tibetan forms (*mirgod*, 'wildman') can also mean 'robber', 'ruffian' or 'thief', and the verb 'to rob' can also mean 'to act the yeti'.

If the religious practices of the Tibetans suggest the existence of a creature which is neither man nor monkey, but akin to both, how does this evidence square with present-day reports from the inhabitants of the Himalayas? Descriptions are mostly obtained from the Sherpas, a tribe comprising at most 1,000 people whose remote homelands were cut off from contact with the West until the 20th-century fashion for mountaineering began. They are a world symbol for good nature and endurance, living by trade and mountain porterage. Mongolian by origin and Nepalese by adoption, they crossed the mountain passes into their current homeland some time during the Middle Ages. The Sherpas have no doubt that the Yeti is a living creature. Their contacts with it apparently take place either in the summer, when small groups of men are guarding their flocks on the snowfield pastures, or during the winter, when both man and Yeti are living at far lower altitudes. The geographic region supposedly frequented by the Yeti is a honeycomb of rugged outcrops, boulder-fields and caves. This, of course, could be one reason why, despite the numerous sightings and footprints, a really first-class well-documented occupation site or live Yeti has not been found.

It is difficult to select representative examples from the literally hundreds of sightings and thousands of reports of tracks and calls. Some of the Yetis have been sighted by Sherpas while they themselves have remained unobserved – the animals being caught eating, sitting on rocks or just walking alone. There is even the story of one man who met a Yeti face to face round a corner of a rock, both being frozen to the spot with fright until the man, recovering breath, pulled a knife and shouted. This story has a curious parallel in Chinese Yeti tales.

There are everyday stories like that of Lakhpa Tensing, a yak herder from Namche Bazaar, who saw a Yeti in March 1951 when he was rounding up a stray yak one evening at dusk. He came upon the corpse of a mouse hare and saw a small Yeti (about the size of a twelve-year-old boy) sitting on a rock with its back to him. Although he was very frightened of it the creature was obviously far more interested in its dinner than in him. Tensing noted that the Yeti had a curious pointed head and red-brown hair.

Pasang Nima (a caravan leader from Tibet who lived near the Nepal border) saw a Yeti one day in a flat area about 200–300 yards away from him. It was about the size and build of a small man, the head covered with long hair but the face and chest not very hairy at all. Reddish-brown in colour and bipedal, it was busy grubbing up roots, and occasionally emitted a loud high-pitched cry.

Do these accounts sound like the products of imagination? To me they seem very reasonable stories which might be told by any group of herders ranging far afield from their villages and acutely aware of the animal life around them. It has, however, been claimed with some fairness that the concentration of sightings in Sherpa country could represent more the willingness of the Sherpa people to supply the desired answer to a visitor's question than it does the actual distribution of the Yeti.

Most Tibetan religious leaders firmly believe in the Yeti. Lord Hunt, admittedly a pro-Yeti advocate as we have seen, quotes the following story told to him by the Abbot of Thyangboche Monastery, which is sufficiently low-key to be believable:[9]

Seated with Charles Wylie and Tensing [Norgay] beside our host, a rotund figure robed in faded red, I questioned him about the Yeti. . . . The old dignitary at once warmed to this subject. Peering out of the window on to the meadow where our tents were pitched, he gave a most graphic description of how a Yeti had appeared from the surrounding thickets, a few years back in the winter when the snow lay on the ground. This beast, loping along sometimes on his hind legs and sometimes on all fours, stood about five feet high and was covered with grey hair, a description which we have heard from other eyewitnesses. . . . The Yeti had stopped to scratch – the old monk gave a good imitation, but went on longer than he need have done to make his point – had picked up snow, played with it and made a few grunts – again he gave us a convincing rendering. The inhabitants of the monastery had meanwhile worked themselves into a great state of excitement and instructions were given to drive off the unwelcome visitor. Conch shells were blown and the long traditional horns sounded. The Yeti ambled away into the bush.

Despite minor regional differences a remarkable similarity exists between many Sherpa accounts (and also many European ones) – remarkable especially since the distances between some of the areas are great and their inhabitants have little contact with each other. A general picture emerges of a large-size unaggressive, apelike, long-armed animal covered in reddish hair. It is nocturnal, omnivorous, with a characteristic high-pitched cry and a conical-shaped head. Nearly three-quarters of the reports say it is only partly bipedal, in other words that when travelling in a great hurry or deep snow it moves on all fours. It has a powerful sense of smell and good eyesight – two reasons, one imagines, why the enormous European expeditions sent to observe, kill or capture specimens have been unsuccessful. Yetis are, curiously, usually observed as solitary individuals, although there are a few cases of multiple sightings and family groups. It has been suggested that the solitaries are old males, temporarily or permanently living apart from the group, since this is a behaviour pattern typical of the orang-utan.

The Yeti habitat is sometimes represented as lifeless and barren and thus (by default) impossible for a Yeti to survive in, whereas actually it is teeming with animal life, not only the mouse hare (little guinea-pig-like rodents), which the Yeti seems to favour, but also other rodents and foxes, as well as insects and grubs in the summer months. In winter these food supplies may run short and the Yeti presumably migrates southwards and downwards, but the stray bharal (blue sheep) and serow may still remain, to be preyed on by Yeti, snow leopard and bear alike. Only above 18,000 ft does the animal and vegetable life begin to thin out, but in a customary range of 12,000–19,000 ft there would be plenty to sustain an omnivorous primate.

11 *A Yeti reconstruction, showing the curious pointed head and clumsy gait.*

It is possible that the main areas of habitation are not these high altitude snowfields, but rather the subtropical intermontane valleys which support a very different fauna and flora. If the densely vegetated areas (like the upper Arun Valley explored in 1972) support the major breeding populations then it may be that we are seeing only the outliers, the Yeti equivalents of hermits and solitaries, away from their normal home ranges. Few Yeti shelters have been found (none have been seen by Europeans), although it has been claimed that the Yeti makes gorilla-like nests, twisting newly-broken juniper branches interwoven to make nesting platforms. It also has small 'lairs' among the rocks, identifiable by its curiously pungent and unpleasant smell and by concentrations of faeces and hair.

Whatever the Yeti's habitat and pattern of life, it is certainly rare, an endangered species. Yeti flesh was much sought after by Buddhist monks as an aphrodisiac and general cure-all; not being allowed to kill, the monks obtained the flesh from caravan merchants who themselves acquired it from local hunters. No doubt these practices contributed in a minor way to the general reduction in Yeti populations reported by local people between the 18th and 20th centuries – the major cause presumably being increasing pressure on Yeti habitats from growing human populations. Like the wild yak (which lives in very much the same kind of territory) the Yeti is part of a relict fauna, and is now apparently more common in China, Kazakhstan and the Pamir Mountains. It could be that in the Himalayas we are seeing only the outliers of the Yeti's natural range, a hypothesis supported by the fact that those observed are usually solitaries.

Scepticism about the exact nature – indeed the existence – of the Yeti would be eliminated if only actual specimens – living or dead – could be scientifically examined. Dead ones are reported. Villagers from Tharbaleh (over the Tibet border), near Rongbuk glacier, once saw a drowned Yeti which had been washed up on rocks, describing it as about the same size as a small man with a pointed head but covered with red-brown hair. Unfortunately the villagers were afraid to keep the creature's skin since, like many Sherpas, they believed that the Yeti brought bad luck. Several Buddhist monasteries of the Everest region, including Pangboche, Thyangboche and Khumjung, keep what are alleged to be Yeti scalps. The Pangboche specimen was first seen by Westerners in 1953, and is the property of the temple in that village, where it was kept stored away with the other trappings and ornaments for the sacred dances. The *Daily Mail* expedition attempted, unsuccessfully, to purchase it or obtain it on loan, but was at any rate able to make a detailed description.

The local Sherpas were positive that the Pangboche scalp was from a Yeti, and the *meh-teh* (manlike) form at that. The object was conical and helmet-shaped, as if made to fit a man's head (which of course it had been), and cut off symmetrically above the ears. It did not seem to have been sewn together, nor at first sight had it been artificially shaped. The outer surface was largely bare and the skin fairly smooth, but in its original state it had been quite clearly covered with reddish hair sloping back from the forehead and downwards on the sides. A prominent crest or 'keel' ran from the base of the forehead upwards over the crown and down the back, covered with bristle-like hairs. Its height was some $7\frac{1}{2}$ in. and length $9\frac{3}{4}$ in. It was made of very uniform thick skin, even thicker than that of the domestic yak. Photographs of the scalp and its hairs were sent to London, where it was suggested that it was merely a piece of skin worked into the shape of the cranium. To dwell on this is, I think, missing the point, as the 'scalp' itself was obviously of great age and had functioned as a true Yeti scalp in the temple rituals *because* the monks – and the Sherpas generally – believed in it, irrespective of the animal from which it originated. By expecting the Pangboche scalp, or any other Yeti scalp for that matter, actually to have been cut from a Yeti skin, we are ignoring the religious beliefs of the monks, who made no distinction between the Yeti itself and the Yeti-actor equipped with this scalp, at least in the temple dances. This theme is a common one in medieval pageants and in tribal dances, like those of the Australian aborigines, where dancers taking the role of a particular animal are imagined actually to become that animal during the ritual of the dance.

The second, even more famous, scalp comes from Khumjung. In size it is markedly similar to the one from Pangboche, and some local legends say that it came from a female Yeti, whereas the Pangboche scalp came from a male. In 1960 Sir Edmund Hillary was able to borrow the Khumjung scalp for six weeks, to have it examined by scientists and exhibited in three countries. The results (apart from the benefits to Khumjung, which included the renovation of the monastery and the building of a new school) suggest that the scalp was made from the shoulder of a serow (*Capricornis sumatraensis*), the Himalayan goat-antelope. But it may not be quite so simple, as some people have pointed out that hairs from the scalp look distinctly monkey-like, and that it contains parasitic mites of a species different from that recovered from the serow. The Khumjung scalp itself is now on exhibition at the monastery, where anyone can see it for a modest ten rupees. The abbot of Thyangboche is firmly convinced that the Yeti exists, and there is certainly no confusion over the nature of the Yeti scalps in the minds of the monks living in these monasteries.

Rumours of further mummified remains abound, and at least one lama (Chemed Rigdzin Dorje) claims that complete mummified Snowmen exist. The only other well-documented relic, a mummified hand also from Pangboche, was studied by Tom Slick's team in the 1950s, but even detailed investigation of small skin samples back in European laboratories failed to reach a diagnosis. Local rumour maintains that the hand comes from a rather poorly mummified high lama, but it has some curiously anthropoid features.

Heuvelmans also gives an account (culled from the *Kathmandu Commoner* of May 1957) of a Yeti head which had been kept for some twenty-five years in the remote village of Chilunka, 50 miles northeast of the capital. Its preservation marked the bravery of its executioners, a party of Nepalese soldiers who had been avenging the death of thirty-one of their companions at the hands of the very same creature, which they caught up with while it was sleeping off the results of such a heavy repast. This is not the only 'evidence' of an encounter with the Yeti at close quarters. In 1948 two Norwegian prospectors, Thorberg and Frostis, were crossing the Zemu gap from Sikkim into east Nepal, when they came across a double set of manlike tracks and eventually upon their makers. An unsuccessful attempt to lasso one resulted, not unreasonably, in the Yeti's attacking; one person was knocked down and mauled while the other escaped. The whole story is redolent of fable.

A Yeti *was* apparently captured once in the 19th century, according to a gentleman in South Africa who heard a radio broadcast of mine about this whole question and wrote in February 1981 to tell me his story:

Many years ago in India my late wife's mother told me how her mother had actually seen what might have been one of these creatures at Mussorie, in the Himalayan foothills. This semi-human was walking upright, but was obviously more animal than human with hair covering its whole body. It was reportedly caught up in the snows and when seen by this lady, covered with skins. This event must have taken place well over a hundred years ago and, of course, I have no further knowledge except that his captors had it in chains. However, I thought this recollection might be of interest to you, for as a result of this episode and other folk-lore my mother-in-law, who was born and bred out there, was a firm believer in the existence of the yeti. I too knew these parts very well and can assure you that there are extensive unexplored and unexplorable areas.

The antiquity of this story – which presumably comes from the late 19th century – is of great importance, since it pre-dates the main era of mountaineering and belongs to a period when few Yeti reports have been noted. It is also significant that both the originator of the report and my correspondent knew the area well, and were presumably acquainted with its flora and fauna. The description of the creature itself makes no mention of size and could, if one discounts the phrase 'more animal than human', refer to a solitary eccentric or a lunatic. The mention of its being 'covered with skins' may also be important, although it is not clear whether the creature had been wearing the skins when captured or was merely draped in them for exhibition, for modesty's sake. If it was the former, then we have not only a documented captured Yeti but also the only reference existing to a Yeti wearing clothes.

Only recently I had another letter, this time from a student at Cambridge who had recently spent some months in India, where she met a pair of well-known travel writers. They have a house in Mussorie, in the Himalayan foothills, and told my correspondent of a Yeti sighting which had been recounted to them in 1961. One evening when having dinner the subject of the Yeti had come up and the writers had asked their servant whether he had ever seen any such strange animals. The man came from one of the more remote of the Himalayan villages and was well acquainted with the local flora and fauna, making it unlikely that he would confuse what he had seen with a langur, or any variety of bear. He was not an educated man and found it very difficult to find the correct words to describe the creature, suggesting that the story is genuine, not fabricated. He described the visit of a large manlike creature which appeared in his village one winter. The villagers, frightened that it would destroy their crops, had it shot by a retired army man and buried in the fields. The creature was naked, covered in reddish hair, but had features which were 'almost human'. The servant was certain that it was not an ape or a bear – and equally certain that he could recall the exact place where the corpse was buried. So, with luck and exhumation, we *might* be able to settle doubts once and for all, but many people have said that before and I am far from optimistic about the outcome.

1  (Above) Thin energetic satyrs at play, from a Greek Red Figure neck amphora.
2  (Centre) Hairless tumescent satyr by the 'Painter of the Woolly Satyrs', from a Greek bell krater.
3  (Below) Some members of the original Russian 'Snowman Commission', formed in 1958. Left to right: Professor P. Smoline, Professor B. F. Porshnev, Professor A. A. Mashkovtsev, Dmitri Bayanov and Dr M.-J. Kofman.

4–7 Medieval wildmen. (Above) Wildman and wildwoman on an English 14th-century manuscript. (Centre) A 16th-century carnival wildman in a skin costume with holes cut at knees and elbows to allow him to move freely. (Opposite above) A 15th-century wildman with a club over the entrance to St Michael's Church, Peasenhall, Suffolk. (Opposite below) Nebuchadnezzar as a wildman: a 15th-century German illustration.

8  John Green, the American Bigfoot investigator, with his collection of outsize footprint casts.

9  The monkey boy of Sri Lanka found in 1973, aged between 10 and 12, living with a family of monkeys in southern Ceylon.

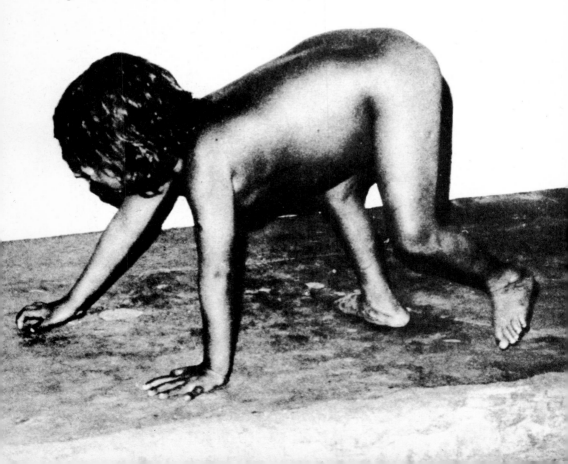

10 Rene Dahinden and Roger Patterson with casts of Bluff Creek Sasquatch footprints from the American northwest.

11 Bigfoot hunter Rene Dahinden and friend – an 8-foot Sasquatch statue by Jim McClarin which stands at Willow Creek, California.

12, 13 (Above) Two stills from the film shot in 1967 by Roger Patterson, which apparently shows a female Sasquatch (nicknamed 'Patti') making off into the woods at Bluff Creek, California. Note the thick shoulders, lack of neck and heavy brow ridges.

14 (Below) Numbar – the top of the montane forest belt and transition to the high snowfields near Everest.

15, 16 (Opposite) Trail of Yeti prints on the Menlung Glacier, Himalayas, November 1951. (Inset) The famous footprint (13 × 18 in.) photographed by Eric Shipton on the same day near the Menlung Glacier – even sceptics find this one difficult to explain away.

17 A Lama from Thyangboche monastery, whose monks have observed
the Yeti for hundreds of years.

18 Sherpa portrait of a Yeti from a large painting showing the village of
Tenboche before the white man arrived.

# Chapter 4
# The Chinese Yeti

The Chinese Yeti first burst upon an unsuspecting Western world in the *Sunday Telegraph* on 22 April 1979, under the dramatic headline, 'Soldiers ate a Yeti'. The article was based on one in the Chinese journal *Huashi* ('Fossils'), which reported that as long ago as 1962 soldiers of the Chinese army operating in an area vaguely described as 'the foothills of the Himalayas' had killed and eaten a 'Yeti-like creature'. The article spoke of the 'meat from a snowman' which the soldiers had killed in a remote part of Yun-an province. At least ten other Yeti sightings had been made since then in and around Tibet, including one as recently as 1976.[1]

A search of *Huashi* reveals that the whole Yeti question had first been mentioned by one Shi Zhu in 1977, under the title, 'Does the wildman exist?', which concentrated on reviewing international 'wildman' stories and is not therefore of specific interest.[2] The next articles from China in English ('Wild Man – fact or fiction?' and 'Shennongjia Forests: home of rare species') are to be found in the July and August 1979 issues of the current affairs magazine *China Reconstructs*.[3] The former article is by far the more important, and is written by researchers at the Institute of Palaeoanthropology and Vertebrate Palaeontology of the Chinese Academy of Sciences, after investigations in northwest Hubei province into the reported existence of wildmen in that area.

Apparently ancient Chinese literary works and folk legends include references to big hairy manlike creatures which live in the vast forests of the Quinling-Bashan-Shennongjia mountain region of central China (northwest Hubei province). The remote and mystical Shennongjia mountains abound in legends; it seems that even Shennong, god-king of fable and father of husbandry and farming, was deterred by their altitude and had to build a scaffolding when he came here to collect medicinal herbs. And that

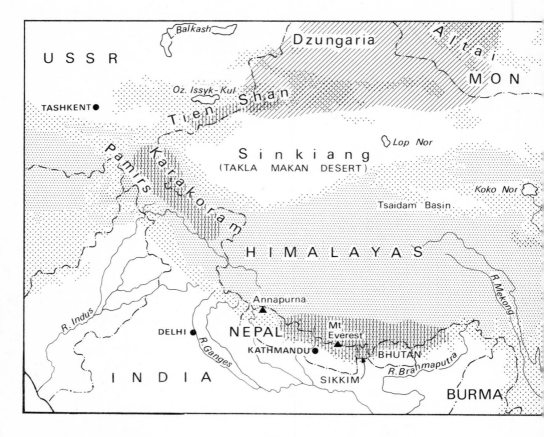

12 *Areas where Yetis and Almas have been sighted in the Himalayas, Outer Mongolia and China (Fangxian county).*

is how the area got its name – from Shennong and the Chinese word *jia* meaning 'scaffold'.

Shennongjia is an area of approximately 1,250 sq. miles, comprising steep, rugged mountains mostly up to 8,200 ft with the highest peaks at 10,000 ft. The mountains above 5,900 ft retain the temperatures of early winter even while the surrounding lowlying hills swelter in July heat, giving a curious microclimate to Shennongjia that has resulted in the growth and survival of a unique and diverse fauna. The area has become one of China's major sources of rare and exotic woods, as well as of desirable 'arrow bamboo' which makes first-quality paper – and provides food for giant pandas.

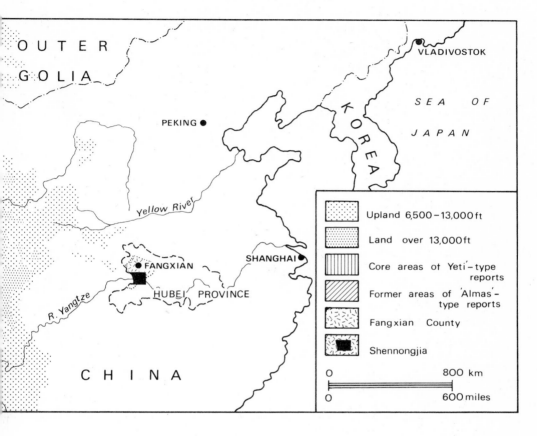

There are early references to the presence of strange primates. Two thousand years ago, during the Warring States period, Qu Yuan (340–278 B C), the statesman-poet of the State of Chu, referred in his verse to 'mountain ogres'. His home was, significantly, just south of Shennongjia, in what is today the Zigui county of Hubei province. In Tang dynasty times (A D 618–907) the historian Li Yanshou in his *Southern History* describes a band of 'hairy men' in the region of modern Jiangling county, also in Hubei. Later still, the Ch'ing dynasty poet, Yuan Mei (1716–98), in his book *New Rhythms* tells of the existence of a creature described as 'monkey-like, yet not a monkey' in southwestern Shaanxi province, Xianning county.

The first scientific observation of a Chinese Yeti was made relatively recently, by a biologist. Wang Zelin graduated from the Faculty of Biology at Northwestern University, Chicago, but

13,14 *Two Chinese hill-monsters from a rich pantheon of similar mythological characters which might ultimately be derived from Yetis.*

狒狒圖

returned to China at the start of the Second World War. In 1940 he was working with the Yellow River Irrigation Committee when he had the following experience:[4]

Around September or October, we were travelling from Baoji to Tianshui via Jiangluo City; our car was between Jiangluo City and Niangniang Plain when we suddenly heard gunshots ahead of us. When the car reached the crowd that surrounded the gunman, all of us got down to satisfy our curiosity. We could see that the 'wildman' was already shot dead and laid on the roadside. The body was still supple and the stature very tall, approximately 2 metres [6 ft 6 in.]. The whole body was covered with a coat of thick greyish-red hair which was very dense and approximately one *cun* [1¼ in.] long. Since it was lying face-down, the more inquisitive of the passengers turned the body over to have a better look. It turned out to be a mother with a large pair of breasts, the nipples being very red as if it had recently given birth. The hair on the face was shorter. The face was narrow with deep-set eyes, while the cheek bones and lips jutted out. The scalp hair was roughly one *chi* [*c.* 1 ft] long and untidy. The appearance was very similar to the plaster model of a female Peking Man [the Chinese *Homo erectus*]. However, its hair seemed to be longer and thicker than that of the ape-man model. It was ugly because of the protruding lips.

According to the locals, there were two of them, probably one male and the other female. They had been in that area for over a month. The 'wildmen' had great strength, frequently stood erect and were very tall. They were brisk in walking and could move as rapidly uphill as on the plain. As such, ordinary folks could not catch up with them. They did not have a language and could only howl.

The fact that Wang Zelin was himself a biologist seems to rule out any possibility that the creature was a bear, or anything else already known to science. The precise location and details of the incident all tend to make it believable, and the description accords well with other sightings.

Then on 14 May 1976 at 1 a.m. the incident occurred which really sparked off interest in the whole wildman question, convincing even some of the most hardened Chinese sceptics. Six cadres from the Shennongjia forestry region were driving along the highway near Chunshuy, a village between Fangxian county and Shennongjia, when they came across a strange tailless creature covered in reddish fur, illuminated in the headlamps of the car. The driver kept the lamps on the creature while the others went forward to investigate, getting a look at it from a distance of only a yard or so. They could say with certainty that it was neither a bear nor any other animal which they had ever seen before, and sent a telegram to the Chinese Academy of Sciences in Peking. This initiated a great degree of public interest, people writing in to report other sightings and groups of scientists and the army mounting expeditions into the forest. Finally it was decided that a proper investigating team must be organized, composed of scientists from Peking, Shanghai and Hubei, Shaanxi and Sichuan provinces, together with photographers and special infiltration teams of soldiers with rifles, tranquillizer dart guns, tape recorders and hunting dogs. The massive team (eventually comprising over 100 members assisted by army scouts from Wuhan) worked in the area during 1976 and 1977, interviewing hundreds of people. Together with local militiamen and commune members, the team organized several large searches, but (as is usual with such expeditions) they found nothing definite. Some significant things did, however, emerge.

On 19 June 1976 Gong Yulan, a thirty-two-year-old member of the Quiaoshang commune in Fangxian county was in the mountains cutting grass, accompanied by her four-year-old child, when they saw a wildman scratching its back against a tree trunk. The team was able to locate the tree which the woman described, and at a height of 4 ft 3 in. from the ground they found several dozen fine hairs. Later investigators examining the tree in August of the same year found two long hairs 5 ft 11 in. from the ground.[5]

During the two-year project an area of 500 sq. miles was investigated, and data on local geology, flora and fauna were collected as well. The only actual traces of the wildmen were hairs, footprints and faeces. Where there were many records of sightings, the descriptions were, as usual, quite standardized. A typical example is that taken from a statement by Wu Jiayan and Niu Yong of the Shaanxi Biological Resources Investigation team in 1977, on the report of a hairy man from the Taibai mountains of central Shaanxi province. They recorded the following account from Pang Gensheng, a thirty-three-year-old team leader from the Cuifeng commune in Shaanxi's Zhouzhi county.

In early June, 1977, I went to Dadi Gully to cut logs. Somewhere between 11 and 12 in the morning I ran into a 'hairy man' in the woods on the slope of the gully. It came closer and closer. I got scared and kept retreating until my back was against a stone cliff and I couldn't go any further. The hairy man came up to seven or eight feet, and then to about five feet from me. I raised my axe, ready to fight for my life. We stood like that, neither of us moving, for more than an hour. Then I groped for a stone and threw it at him. It hit him in the chest. He uttered several howls and rubbed the spot with his left hand. Then he turned left and leaned against a tree, then walked away slowly towards the bottom of the gully. He kept making a mumbling sound. He was about seven feet tall [a Chinese foot is 33 cm – not 30.5 cm as in our system] with shoulders wider than a man's, a sloping forehead, deep-set eyes, and bulbous nose with slightly upturned nostrils. He had sunken cheeks, ears like a man's but bigger, and round eyes also bigger than a man's. His jaw jutted out and he had protruding lips. His front teeth were as broad as a horse's. His eyes were black. His hair was dark brown and more than a foot long, and hung loosely over his shoulders. His whole face, except for the nose and ears, was covered with short hairs. His arms hung down to below his knees. He had big hands about half a foot long and with thumbs only slightly separated from the fingers. He didn't have any tail, and the hair on his body was short. He had thick thighs, shorter than the lower part of his leg. He walked upright with his legs apart. His feet were each about a foot long and half that broad – broader in front and narrow behind, with splayed toes. He was a male. That much I saw clearly.

This account both agrees and disagrees in details with other descriptions of the Yeti. General bodily proportions, hairiness, length of arms and so on are very similar, and the foot shape has also been mentioned in connection with both the Himalayan Yeti and the North American Bigfoot. The distribution of body hair is interesting since these creatures are more often described as having hairless faces. The curious propensity of the Chinese Yetis for leaning against trees has resulted in the accumulation of a large amount of their hair. Other features of the accounts which seem peculiar to China are the occasional aggressiveness (or just curiosity) which the creatures exhibit, and their wide range of sounds (in this account, for example, the creature both mumbles and howls). Of course the cry of the Yeti has been described in a variety of different ways and folktales contain references to the Yeti's being able to mimic the call of any animal, but these mumblings and howlings have a fairly authentic ring.

A bastardized version of this last story appeared in the 15 June 1981 edition of the British magazine *Weekend*, which carried, under the headline 'Hairy Encounter', a brief account of the sighting in Shaanxi province by 'Pong Ke-Shem' ( = Pang Gensheng):

It was a good 10′ tall [the magazine does not state whether this is Chinese or English measurement] and hairy all over. It had thick lips and big teeth, like a horse's. It was covered in long, brown hair and its arms were very long and its feet were huge. I was terrified and flung a rock at its leg, but instead of rushing at me it uprooted a small tree and, using it as a walking stick, limped away!

This is a splendid example of the way a story can be distorted in the reporting.

An even more curious incident was reported in the *Daily Telegraph* for 2 December 1980 under the sensational title, 'Chinese Child Fathered by Apeman'. The *Telegraph*'s special correspondent in Peking had read in the official daily paper (*Guangming*) an account of a woman who had disappeared for twenty-seven days in 1939 in 'a forest area frequented by the "wild men of Hupen [Hubei]" province'. The mountainous area referred to is clearly Shennongjia, and the human interest of the story stems from the fact that the woman claimed she was captured by 'wildmen' and later gave birth to a 'monkey child', a somewhat curious circumstance at any time but made even more interesting since, although admitting to having been captured by apemen, she 'denied having any relations with them'. The offspring of this dubious union, the so-called 'monkey child' of the headline, died in 1960 aged twenty-one, but its bones, according to the *Guangming* daily, have recently been dug up, and examination showed that 'the child's skeleton had the characteristics of an ape and a man'. How frustrating not to have a proper scientific report on this skeleton, even if the flavour of the story makes one approach the incident with a certain measure of caution! Still, considerable public interest in the Chinese Yeti was now aroused, and it occasioned mention in scientific circles.

Zhou Guoxing, an anthropologist with the Peking Museum of Natural History, presented the findings of his study of the Yeti at a conference commemorating the fiftieth anniversary of the discovery of Peking Man. The only reference to this in Western papers occurs in yet another sensationally-headlined article, this time in *The New York Times* for 5 January 1980, under the banner 'It's Tall, It Has Wavy Hair and Chinese Keep Hunting for It'. Mr Zhou has apparently published a dozen or so popular books on archaeology and anthropology and had been put in charge of scientific research for the 1977 expedition to Shennongjia. No creatures were captured but much evidence of their existence was gleaned. At one point the expedition search party moved near to one of the creatures; unfortunately 'before the beast could be captured an anxious soldier accidentally shot himself in the leg. The shot brought expedition members scurrying in from all directions and presumably frightened the creature away.'[6]

In 1981 there appeared this very strange report in the 19 January edition of the *Peking Evening News*, also from Shennongjia:[7]

### New Information about the 'Wild Men' –
### A Report from Shennongjia by Peng Hengcai

The first year of the planned five-year investigation into the strange creatures of northwest Hubei Province which has attracted worldwide attention is drawing to a close. Members of the investigation teams have come in from Zhushan, Fang Xian, Dawan and other places and assembled at the centre of the investigation – Songbai in Shennongjia forest.

During 1980 the investigating teams, enduring hunger and exposure and triumphing over severe difficulties, have uncovered new material and made important discoveries about the mysterious 'wildmen'. During this year, each team has discovered quantities of material evidence of these strange creatures including tracks, hair and faeces. 150 *li* [47 miles] from the main peak of Shennongjia, on Mount Quiangdao at 2,400 m [7,900 ft] above sea level, they discovered on two separate occasions a total of over two hundred footprints made by the strange creatures. The footprints discovered on the first occasion were 48 cm [*c.* 19 in.] in length, with an average stride of 2.5 m [8 ft 3 in.], the largest footprints so far discovered anywhere in the world. These continuous, distinct, firm footprints, in which the five toes clearly stand out, have been filmed by the Central News Film Unit.

During 1980 members of the public from, amongst other places, Shaanxi and Sichuan provinces have given many eyewitness accounts of 'wildmen' to the investigators. Yan Mingde, an elderly peasant from Bancang No.2 Brigade, Bancang Commune, told an investigation team that during the ninth lunar month [October-November] of 1947, while he was a conscript in the KMT [Nationalist] army, eight red-haired wildmen ran out of the virgin forest at Yangjiaodong [Ram's Horn Cave] and were pursued by over two thousand soldiers for more than ten days. Eventually the eight wildmen took refuge in a hermit's cottage deep in the mountains. The soldiers surrounded the three-roomed thatched hut, put up machine guns and set fire to the building, whereupon seven huge wild men over eight *chi* [7 ft 10 in.] tall lifted up the rafters and thatch and broke through the encirclement. A small one was left behind; he had stumbled and fallen into the inferno and been burned. He was caught and hacked to pieces in the open. Yan Mingde's account of the largest group of 'wildmen' ever recorded in northwest Hubei is a highly significant new discovery.

Not long ago, Liao Conggui and his nephew were cutting firewood at Dayanwu. Because it was very misty, they kept calling out to one another, which attracted two 'wildmen'. After this incident an investigation team found at the scene of the event large numbers of distinct footprints 39 cm [15¼ in.] in length, together with other convincing evidence.

During a year of practical investigation, the investigating teams have established something of the lifestyle of the strange creatures. Analysis of consistent eye-witness accounts suggests that they have very probably abandoned the life-mode of diurnal activity in order to reduce the threat posed to them by mankind. The teams have also concluded that peripatetic group investigation is a major cause of low efficiency in investigative work and is not suitable for their purposes.

The first part of the report, containing the descriptions of the huge footprints, actually made world news on 20 January 1981. Yet the story of the eight red-haired wildmen strikes me as fable. The third incident, the sighting of two wildmen by woodcutters, is much more credible, especially as the sighting was backed up by footprints. But one of the most significant features of the report is the low-key comment at the end, confirming a suggestion which some scientists (including myself) have been making for years – that a small party of people staying in one place for a long time will be the only possible way of obtaining definitive scientific information about these creatures. Valuable parallels may be drawn here between the large and expensive operations to track the Yeti in China and Nepal, and the smaller but infinitely more rewarding studies of the mountain gorilla by Dian Fossey, or of chimpanzee behaviour by Jane van Lawick-Goodall.

One can propose the following hypotheses to account for the Chinese Yeti:

1   Everything is invented and these creatures do not exist.
2   These creatures *do* exist and are either a previously unknown or a previously unclassified variety of primate.

3   Other possibilities, such as 'throwbacks' to primitive types, men who have literally 'gone wild', hermits/idiots living in wild places.

If hypothesis 2 is accepted, the question of classification remains, and in order to solve that it would be necessary to compare behaviour and skeletal/morphological characteristics with other primates. There is no question of the Chinese Yeti being manlike, since it does not resemble *Homo* in any way. At least in China the remains of hairs and faeces have been found, but hair analysis and description are notoriously difficult. The Peking scientists were only able to say conclusively that their Yeti hairs were very different indeed from either brown or black bear. Four other primates live in Shennongjia, and the next stage is clearly to compare their hairs. Many thousands of footprints were found, most of which turned out to be from bears or similar animals, but some were highly peculiar. These were of elongated feet (exact measurements of length are not recorded in the literature), 4 in. wide in front and narrower (*c.* 2 in.) at the back, with the toe marks oval in shape and one toe rather separated from the others. When the footprints followed each other in single file the distance between varied from $19\frac{1}{2}$ in. to 39 in.

Some faeces were also found in September 1976,[8] little piles of dung on top of a steep rock halfway up a mountain in the Hongta commune of Fangxian county. During the period before and after this find, four wildmen sightings were made in the area and on three occasions, March, May and July 1976, these involved a female and its child. In the November of that same year a single adult was seen. The faeces (very much dried out) were similar to those of human beings and contained bits of undigested fruit skins and wild chestnuts, but no animal fur or bones. This is interesting and probably significant, since *Gigantopithecus*, a possible Yeti ancestor, was primarily a vegetarian, as is the mountain gorilla, whose habitat resembles Shennongjia in many ways. However, other faeces found on 30 August 1977 at Tielu Gully in the Panshui commune, Shennongjia, came from a hill slope and a cave, and suggested a more varied diet. They contained the remains of insect cocoons, and had been obtained by investigators following a wildman's footprint trail where the creature had apparently stopped at one point to dig insect cocoons out of the bark of birch trees and eat them. The faeces closely resembled those of an omnivorous large primate, and differed markedly from those of either bears or hoofed animals. The most likely possibilities are that the Yeti represents either another branch of the primate family tree,

*15 Gigantopithecus – a giant ape which possibly became extinct half a million years ago and which may be the ancestor of the Yeti.*

or a supposedly extinct species sharing a common ancestor with other primates (for example, the mountain gorilla) and, ultimately, with man himself.

The Chinese incline towards the view that their creature is related to *Gigantopithecus*. *Homo* and *Gigantopithecus* were probably descended from common stocks which diverged about 20 million years ago, but then underwent certain evolutionary stages broadly in parallel.[9] The taxonomy of *Gigantopithecus* is uncertain – it is known only from a few teeth and fossil jawbones from China and India[10] – but apparently it was a large, ground-feeding, apelike genus about the size of a modern gorilla, with molar teeth well adapted to crushing tough material and flattened canines. It seems more plausible that the Yeti is a descendant rather than actually a living representative of *Gigantopithecus*. *Gigantopithecus* is supposed to have died out half a million years ago, but he or his descendants could possibly still survive. The coelocanth was once supposed to be extinct, yet is now known to be very much alive. The Shennongjia region is full of plants referred to as 'living fossils', including the metasequoia, the dove tree and the Chinese tulip tree, and rare animals have also been found there – a white bear, the giant panda, the takin, and the golden monkey, three varieties of which have now been identified from this region, the only part of the world where they are found. My own view is that this unique flora and fauna provide the perfect refuge for an unknown primate, whether *Gigantopithecus* himself or his descendant.

There is, however, an alternative (if less scientific) hypothesis. The first Chinese emperor, Hwang-Ti, builder of the Great Wall, may have had an unwitting hand in Yeti-making. According to an ancient legend, some people tried to avoid compulsory labour on the wall by taking to the forests and hiding there where, even after many generations, their descendants became wild, large and hairy but retained the power of speech. They emerged periodically from the forest and enquired, 'Has the wall been finished yet?'. But, although the answer was 'Yes', they didn't believe it and returned to the forest where, alas, reality is about to catch up with them.

# Chapter 5
# Almas
# in Mongolia

Ivan Ivlov, a Russian children's doctor, was travelling in the Altai mountains of southern Mongolia in 1963 when he saw a family of manlike creatures consisting of a male, female and a small child, standing on a mountain slope. Ivlov is a man of high reputation whose father, Nicholai, was also a doctor and worked in the Mongolian capital Ulan Bator for many years; indeed, there is actually a monument erected to his memory. So we are not dealing with folktales or local legends, but with an event which was recorded by a trained scientist and transmitted to the proper authorities. There is no reason to doubt Ivlov's word, partly because of his impeccable scientific reputation and partly because, although he had heard local stories about these creatures he had remained sceptical about their existence. Ivlov was able to observe this particular family of 'Almas' – as they are called in Mongolia – through field glasses at a distance of about half a mile for some time, until they moved off and disappeared from view behind a jutting rock. The Mongol driver who accompanied him also saw the creature, assuring him that they were quite common in the area.[1]

Much surprised by this event, Ivlov had the idea of questioning the children who were his patients, reasoning that their accounts were less likely to be biassed than those of adults. He found that many of them had seen Almas, and obtained a number of detailed stories. One child told him of a time when he had seen a male Almas crossing the shallow waters of a creek where he and a whole group of other children had been bathing. The Almas had been accompanied by an Almas child, which it put upon its shoulders to wade across the river, taking no notice of the group of human children who were looking at it with amazement but not, apparently, with any fear. Ivlov's small patient told him that they could all see the back of the male Almas quite clearly, and the little Almas child looking over its shoulder, sticking its tongue out and making faces at them! This seems a surprising story for any child to invent, especially as it was corroborated by other local people, and Ivlov concluded that it was probably true.

So who, or what, are these Almas who are to be seen strolling so casually across Outer Mongolia, and what is known about them?

In Mongolian the word Almas is a genderless noun meaning a strange species between man and ape, but it might also come from two Mongolian words, *ala* ('to kill') and *mal* ('animals'). Linguists are very undecided on the precise origin of the term, which may also be translated as 'wildman', although the literary Mongolian name *kümün görögesü* is also used with the same meaning, if only by the western Mongols who live in Sinkiang, south of the border of the Mongolian People's Republic. Mongolia is full of place-names associated with Almas, such as *Almasyn dobo* (the hills of Almas), *Almasyn ulan oula* (the red mountains of Almas), *Almasyn ulan khada* (the red rocks of Almas), but the names seem to be confined to the southern regions of Mongolia (the Altai and Gobi junction area) and to parts of Dzungaria over the Russian border.

The difference between Almas stories and those describing, say, the Yeti of the Himalayas or Sasquatch/Bigfoot of North America is the general lack of mythological overtones except in the northwest of the country. Here some mythological elements have been tacked on, and there is also a link with the 'wild hunter' legends of Europe (Chapter 1). In the shamanist legends of northwest Mongolia[2] the souls of the wildmen help the hunters pursue wild beasts in the hope that they will gain some of the results. Some local mythologies include an Almas 'god' to whom is offered only the meat of wild animals and edible wild roots, but this seems to be connected with Buddhist beliefs about the demons who live in mountain forests and highland plateaux. Mongol ethnologists see these myths as being founded on fact, representing a folk tradition of humanlike hairy bipeds who were explained away as demons by some of the early shamans. The legends include references to the fact that the creatures used stone tools and ate only wild foods, and had an aversion to the food of the nomadic cattle-breeders. The Almas are not usually endowed with supernatural powers and the local people are not afraid of them.³ They are regarded as different, more primitive, forms of man whose presence in an area is hardly a cause for remark. There is no evidence that Almas have ever intentionally harmed modern man, although there are plenty of instances where they have deliberately sought to contact him.

Almas stories go back a very long way, but obviously the further back one goes the more difficult it becomes to distinguish what is a genuine literary reference to Almas from the general run of 'wild man of the woods' stories. However, some descriptions from the Tien Shan mountain area (apparently the heartland of Almas stories), which lies to the west of the main Mongolian Altai, date from the 15th century and appear to refer to Almas. These descriptions occur in the remarkable memoirs of a Bavarian nobleman, Hans Schiltberger, who was taken prisoner by the Turks and sent to Timur Lang (Tamerlaine of legend, then Khan of the Golden Horde), destined for the retinue of a Tartar (Mongol) prince named Egidi. Schiltberger managed to return home in about 1427, and wrote a journal of his travels which was completed in 1430 and is now lodged in Munich.⁴ The following extract is taken from this journal, and the Arbus mountains mentioned are to be identified with the Tien Shan range.⁵ Tschekra was a Mongol prince.

Tschekra joined Egidi on his expedition to Siberia, which it took them two months to reach. In that country there is a range of mountains called Arbus which is thirty-two days' journey long. The inhabitants say that beyond the mountains is the beginning of a wasteland which lies at the edge of the earth. No one can survive there because the desert is populated by so many snakes and tigers. In the mountains themselves live wild people, who have nothing in common with other human beings. A pelt covers the entire body of these creatures. Only the hands and face are free of hair. They run around in the hills like animals and eat foliage and grass and whatever else they can find. The lord of the territory made Egidi a present of a couple of forest people, a man and a woman. They had been caught in the wilderness, together with three untamed horses the size of asses and all sorts of other animals which are not found in German lands and which I cannot therefore put a name to.

The interest of this piece is twofold. Firstly, Schiltberger reports that he saw the creatures *with his own eyes*. Secondly, he refers to Przewalski horses, which were only rediscovered by Nicholai

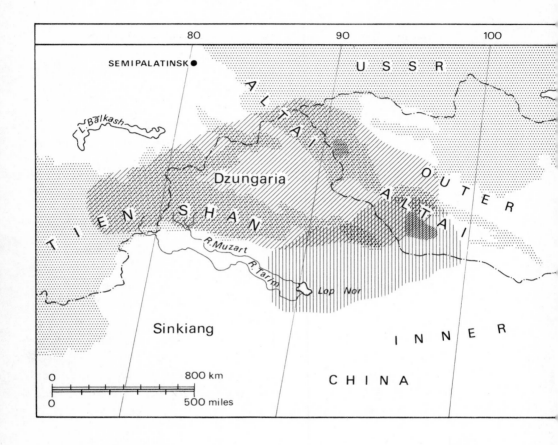

16 *The distribution of reports of Almas in Mongolia and Dzungaria from the 14th century until the present day.*

Przewalski in 1881. The description of the people is vague and they are not named, but the geographical location of the find suggests that this may indeed be the earliest reference to Almas. Przewalski himself saw 'wildmen' in Mongolia in 1871, and legends concerning their presence in Central Asia have been common since the Middle Ages.

After Schiltberger's report virtually nothing is recorded except in some lamaistic ritual paintings, until the Czech anthropologist, Emmanuel Vlček, began work in the 1950s on two old anthropological and anatomical works held in the library of the Gandan monastery in what is now Ulan Bator, the capital of the Mongolian

Legend:
- Reports of Almas from this area C14-20
- Reports of wild camel in late C18
- Current range of wild camel
- Land over 6,500 ft

People's Republic. The first book, published at the end of the 18th century in Peking, included a systematic discussion of the wild fauna of Mongolia and, greatly to Vlček's surprise, contained an unmistakable drawing of a wildman. The book was Tibetan in type, printed from woodcuts on narrow strips of paper, and included an illustration of the creature, which is obviously bipedal, standing upright on a rock and with one arm stretched upwards. It is almost entirely covered with hair, except for the hands and feet, but is not very realistic, being stylized according to the artistic traditions of state lamaism. Trilingual captions say the creature was called *samdja* (Tibetan), *bitchun* (Chinese) and *Kümchin görügösü* (Mongolian), all of which may be translated as 'man-animal'.[6] Further searches in the central library of the Scientific Committee in Mongolia produced a more recent edition of the same

17 (Opposite) A Mongolian Almas from an 18th-century Tibetan
manuscript, showing the figure standing on a rock with one arm raised.
The caption (in Tibetan, Chinese and Mongolian) means 'Wildman'.
18 (Above) The same figure in a later edition of the same book, published
in Ulan Bator.

book, reprinted a century later in Urga (modern Ulan Bator) under the same title, which could be translated as 'Anatomical Dictionary for Recognizing Various Diseases'. Here this same bipedal primate appears as part of a systematic discussion about Mongolian natural history, but some explanatory notes are added in Tibetan to the effect that the given names, here *osodrashin* (Tibetan), *Peeyi* (Chinese) and *zerleg khoon* (Mongolian), are to be taken to mean 'wildman'. The illustration is very similar to the one in the earlier edition, but more stylized and perhaps less credible. The head is covered with hair and the face sports a full beard. The rest of the body, except the hands and feet, has short fur which emphasizes the muscles, particularly the exceptionally well-developed chest – the same features that are also to be seen in Neanderthals (Chapter 9). The Tibetan text beside the picture says: 'The wild man lives in the mountains, his origins close to that of a bear, his body resembles that of man, and he has enormous strength. His meat may be eaten to treat mental diseases and his gall cures jaundice'.

It is particularly interesting that this creature, which is clearly an Almas, must have been sufficiently well known to travellers between Tibet and Mongolia to have been included in what is really a standard work on Mongolian natural history, as it may be applied to Buddhist medicine. The book contains thousands of illustrations of various classes of animals (reptiles, mammals and amphibia), but not one single mythological animal such as are known from similar medieval European books. All the creatures are living and observable today. There seems no reason at all to suggest that the Almas did not also exist, and the supporting text and illustration seem to suggest that it was found among rocky habitats, in the mountains. The distinguished Mongolian scholar, the late Professor Y. Rinchen,[7] said that this book (perhaps more correctly entitled *The Mirror of Medicine*) was written by a Mongol savant called Dondubjaltsan (1792–1855). Although Vlček apparently saw only these two editions, a total of three are now known to exist: an Inner Mongolian edition, the edition of the Tibetan Gumbum monastery and the Mongol edition of the Pandita Geuguen monastery which reproduces the old manuscript with additions in Tibetan, Mongolian, Manchu and Chinese and came from the library of His Holiness the last living Buddha of Urga (modern Ulan

Bator) in 1924. The first drawing published by Vlček comes from the old Inner Mongolian edition and the second from the 1912 revision.

If we accept this as evidence that Almas are (or were) living creatures, then we need to examine the evidence produced by contemporary studies, as well as the documentary records kept in the recent past. Easily the most fascinating of these are the writings of the eccentric and enigmatic Professor Rinchen, whose chequered career and colourful personality made him *persona non grata* in Mongolia during some periods of his life. His rich and varied fund of stories have been quoted with respect and admiration by everyone from nomadic herdsmen to fellow members of the Academy of Sciences.

In 1958 Christopher Dobson, a journalist on assignment in Mongolia, recorded the following description of the Rinchen *ménage*:[8]

One day, walking through the forest, I came upon a 'yurt' – a Mongolian tent – where a plump, middle-aged Mongolian woman was washing clothes by the river. I said 'good morning' to her. And to my utter amazement she said in perfect English 'Good morning, would you like to come for a cup of coffee?'

I had stumbled on the summer home of Dr. Rinchen, Mongolia's best known man of letters. And what a charming man he is.

*19 A reconstruction of the supposed sleeping position of the Dzungarian Almas drawn by the Soviet zoologist Khakhlov in the early 1900s.*

Bronzed and fit, he has a leonine head with a mane of white hair and
Mongolian side whiskers.

We talked there in the middle of an ancient forest on a sacred
mountain, of art and literature of ancient Mongolia. It was then
that I found he was an expert on the Abominable Snowman. 'We
call them Almas, which means wild man' he said.

Forgetting this reference to Abominable Snowmen – apparently
the only explanation that journalists can envisage for 'wildmen' –
we have a charming picture of Rinchen at home. Much of his early
work (he was a linguist) remains uncontested, but he seems to have
fallen from grace and been labelled a 'bourgeois nationalist' before
his death in 1977. Rinchen studied the Almas question for the best
part of fifty years and was indisputably one of the Mongolian
People's Republic's leading intellectuals at the time of his death.

20, 21 *Two reconstructions of the head of a Dzungarian Almas. The original (opposite) comes from Khakhlov's description of 1914, which has also been used to make the second (drawn by the author above), far more 'human' in appearance.*

Rinchen was not, however, the first scholar to observe the Almas; that honour belongs to Badzare Baradyine (sometimes spelt Baradiyn, or Baradiin), who spent April 1906 in the desert of Alachan. One evening, just before sunset when it was time to make camp for the night, the caravan leader suddenly cried out in fear. The caravan stopped, and everyone could see the silhouette of a hairy man standing on top of a hill of sand outlined against the sunset. After examining its visitors for a moment it turned on its heels and disappeared among the dunes, eluding pursuit. This observation provoked great interest in Russian academic circles, but was also greeted with some incredulity and, in the report of his expedition which was published in 1908, Baradyine was requested by no less a person than the president of the Imperial Russian Geographical Society not to publish his account of the incident. Baradyine did, however, tell it to his friend, the eminent Mongolian professor Zhamtsarano, together with other Almas encounters related by his Mongol companions.

Zhamtsarano, a Buryat Mongol, was born in 1880 and was an enthusiastic collector of Mongoliana all his life, surviving banishment to Outer Mongolia (by the Tsarist government, because of his nationalism), and exile (by Soviet authorities) *from* Outer Mongolia *to* Leningrad because of his nationalist attitudes![9] He did extensive fieldwork from the end of the 19th century until 1928 with the object of verifying the Almas stories, and plotted each find on a special map together with the names of his informants. These generally tended to be the itinerant Mongol nomads who crossed the region and reported frequent sightings and a number of footprints. Each date of a sighting was recorded and Zhamtsarano asked the artist Soeltai who accompanied him to make a colour picture from each individual description. This archive has alas since been lost.

Baradyine was arrested and executed for political reasons in 1928/9, and Zhamtsarano himself was, at that time, also in disgrace, although he has since been rehabilitated. It is worth considering how much of the observations of Baradyine and the vast archive of Zhamtsarano would have been available to research workers at later periods – to Rinchen, for example, and later on to Boris Porshnev. Both Baradyine and Zhamtsarano came from the same area and were near-contemporaries (funds were raised for them to be sent to a Russian university by the same local committee on the same day).[10] Zhamtsarano died in 1940, and collections of his papers are held in two archives, 148 items in the collection of the Leningrad Section of the Institute of Oriental Studies of the Academy of Sciences of the USSR,[11] and 31 items in the Institute of Social Sciences of the Buryat Branch of the Siberian Section of the Academy[12] and housed at Ulan Ude. Not readily accessible to the West, one might think, but surely consulted by Soviet scientists?

When Porshnev was doing his research in 1958/9 Zhamtsarano officially did not exist, and although his manuscripts form one of the largest collections in the Leningrad Section of the Institute of Oriental Studies his name was not mentioned in the published descriptions of this Section's archives.[13] Rinchen, however, tells us in his list of Zhamtsarano's work[14] that he had looked at the archive in 1958, the year before he wrote about it. By 1960–62 Zhamtsarano was rehabilitated and several articles appeared celebrating the eightieth anniversary of his birth. Porshnev, however, seems to have been unable to consult this archive, and there are two comments in his published work (one in 1963, one in 1968) indicating that he thought the archive had been destroyed or disappeared. Detective work on the part of a colleague suggests that the archive is still there, but that Rinchen never told Porshnev about it, despite their common interest in the Almas question. This *could* be because the archive does not contain anything on Almas or it could be because Rinchen was anti-Russian. Anyway it looks now as though even Rinchen himself did not go through the full archive, as his lists comprise vague references such as 'Ms in Mongolian' without any further details. The archive includes Zhamtsarano's diaries and field notes for the 1920s when he was doing his great Almas map and survey – it is of incalculable value, but until now everyone has assumed that, like so much other early material, it had simply disappeared. One of the members of his expeditions, Dordji Meiren, described some of the results and these fragments are all that is at present available from Zhamtsarano's trips.

Meiren, who lived in the Gobi area and was a member of the Academy of Sciences, recalled that during the period 1807–67 Almas were reported from Khalkha, the Galbin Gobi and Dzakh Soudjin Gobi as well as from Inner Mongolia. They were especially numerous in the Gourban Bogdin Gobi, Chardzyn Gobi, the Alachan desert (where Rinchen reports very recent sightings) and numerous other places. According to Meiren their numbers had decreased dramatically by 1867–1927, and after this date they seem almost to have disappeared except from the province of Khovd and the southern Gobi. The Mongol hunters themselves concluded that the Almas were becoming very scarce. Meiren said that in 1937 he saw an Almas' skin in one of the Gobi monasteries. It was being used by the lamas as a ritual carpet for some of their ceremonies. The hairs on the skin were reddish and curly, and the skin had been prepared after death by cutting it down the spine, so the chest and face were preserved. The features were hairless, the face had eyebrows, and the head still had long disordered hair. Fingers and toes were in a good state of preservation and the nails were similar to human nails.

The Zhamtsarano story does not quite end here, as the professor earned himself the distinction of becoming immortalized in a novel – the first science-fiction story ever written on this theme. It was called *The Ravine of Almas* by M. Rozenfeld, published in English in 1936 and translated into Russian in 1937 by V.A. Schneiderov.[15] The same author also published a non-fictional account of *A car drive across Mongolia* in Russian in 1930, and discussed many of the Almas stories, citing as a witness Professor Baradyine.

The description of the Almas said to be from these various archives varies only a little in the different regions. Their height is similar to that of modern Mongols (5 ft 3 in.–5 ft 7 in.), but they *seem* shorter because they often walk with their knees semi-flexed. Their jaws are massive, their chins recede, their eyebrow ridges are very prominent compared with those of the Mongols, and the females have long breasts which, when they are sitting on the ground, they can toss over their shoulders to feed the infant that is clinging to their back. These long breasts were noted by Ivlov in the recent sighting (1963) described at the beginning of this chapter.

Some reports also say that the feet are slightly bent inwards, and other people note that the Almas can run very fast and are incapable of making fire. They are frequently reported to be primarily nocturnal, timid, unaggressive and unsociable. They eat both vegetable and animal food, principally small mammals. They do not have an articulate language and they seem incapable of uttering more than a few word-like sounds. One account, seemingly concerned with an incident in the 19th century, described how some Almas took possession of a temporarily deserted camp, warming themselves by the fire and looting dried fruits. They left containers of wine untouched and did not think to put more fuel on the dying fire, nor did they show any aggression when the owners of the camp returned, but retreated harmlessly.

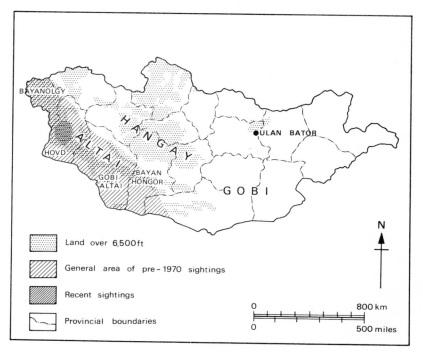

22 *Recent sightings of Almas in Outer Mongolia.*

Another story, which was also reported by Ivlov, is intrinsically even more interesting than his own sighting but, alas, much more dubious. It was told to him as a great secret by a local teacher, who had been hiking in the mountains when he was captured by two female Almas and led away to a group of the creatures who lived in a cave in the mountains. He was closely examined by the creatures, who evinced great curiosity about his clothes and equipment, but he was not harmed. They brought him food, including the carcass of an ibex which they cut up using sharp stones. The teacher said that he was able to make fire to cook this meat by using his magnifying glass, but that the Almas ate it raw. He remained with them for some time (about two weeks) until they lost interest in him, enabling him to escape. How nice it would be to believe this account – one of the few to mention tool-using by the Almas – but to my mind the very fact that it was told by a teacher, a man who presumably knew from his books that hominids used tools, makes it suspect. This is either the most significant of all the

Almas stories or a hoax. The teacher was very secretive about the story and it was not widely known, Ivlov having been chosen as the recipient because of the high degree of respect in which he was held by the local people. The parallels with the supposed kidnapping of Albert Ostman by a Sasquatch (Chapter 2) are striking, even down to the reluctance with which the story was eventually told.

Rinchen collated the early accounts and reported that in the Gobi area both males and females were seen. Small Almas children were also noticed, sometimes alone and sometimes with their mothers, indicating that the populations were large enough to survive and reproduce. The first foreign hunters had fun shooting Almas which did not run away, but this practice was stopped by the locals. There was even a place called *Almasin dobo* (Almas burial), marking the site of one of these episodes. One of Rinchen's main conclusions was that over this long period the areas where Almas were reported was constantly shrinking as a result of increased human activity and the opening-up of parts of Mongolia by the trans-Mongolian railway connecting Peking with Irkutsk in Russia. It has been observed that the distribution of wild horses and camels is also shrinking for the same reasons, with a marked tendency for them to retreat into the remoter western areas.[16] Rinchen considered that the present-day distribution of Almas is limited to about 400 square miles in remote mountain regions at the junction of the Khovd and Bayanolgy provinces,[17] rich in edible fruits and berries and still the natural habitat of moufflon, chamois and snow leopard. During 1962 a Mr Damdin from the State Museum (Ulan Bator) spent several months in this area, returning with sufficient information to justify a second trip in 1963. He recorded many eye-witness accounts during this period from a wide variety of people: members of peasant cooperatives, hunters, students, teachers, and army officers. The following story (in verbatim translation) was told by Mr Choijoa, a Mongol Torgut who originally came from Sinkiang and was a worker at the fruit-growing experimental station run by the Mongolian Academy of Sciences at Bulgan:[18]

It was happened at about ten o'clock of 26th June 1953. I remembered the time, day and month because this event had utterly surprised myself and was engraved on my heart.

At dawn of that day I went to search my lost camels in the direction of so called Red Mountain of Almases. It was a beautiful sunny morning when I dropped into the ravines. The wind spread a fragrance of highland flowers and herbs but I was in hurry to leave before a midday heat this labyrinth of canyons and ravines. My camel climbed up and down in craggy defile. Suddenly I saw in the corner of secluded ravine under two small ammodendron bushes something of camel-colour. I approached and saw a hairy corpse of a robust humanlike creature dried and half-buried by sand. I had never seen such humanlike being covered by camel-colour brownish-yellow short hairs and I recoiled, although in my native land in Sinkiang I had seen many dead men killed in battle. But who was this strange dead thing – man or beast? I decided to return back and thoroughly examine it. I approached once more and looked down from my camel. The dead thing was not a bear or ape and at the same time it was not a man like Mongol and Kazakh or Chinese and Russian. The hairs of its head were longer than on its body. The skin on groin and armpits was darkened and shrivelled like a hide of dead camel.

I have also examined a terrain near this body and never found any rests or wears. Fear seized my heart. I remembered the old tales of Vetala-vampires and thought I was to see before me one of them. And I hurried away. After my return home I had informed our local administration and Mr. Chimeddorje, manager of Fruit Growing Station, but anyone gave attention on my account. And only after ten years I heard from a man, who came from Ulanbator specially for research about Almases, that the dead body in question had a great scientific value – told Mr. Choijoa.

Reputable accounts of Almas are still being recorded. In a 1980 issue of the illustrated bi-monthly magazine *Mongolie*, printed in English but very rarely found in the West, there appeared an article (anonymous) called 'Again the Snowman' which described Almas-sightings from the early 1970s. The most interesting aspects of this short article are firstly the occurrence of a new name, *hun gurees* ('man-beast'), and secondly confirmation that the distribution areas are now very small, restricted to minute parts of Khovd and Bayanolgy provinces (fig. 22), confirming Rinchen's gloomy assessment of prospects for the Almas expressed in 1964. A vague reference to the fact that eye-witnesses are supposed to have testified that the Almas were usually seen in *groups* is also interesting, especially as the information is supposed to have been collected by staff members of the Mongolian Academy of Sciences and is presumably reliable. The trans-Altai steppes (Dzungaria, fig.

16) are also mentioned as former areas of sightings, but specific details are given of encounters by sixteen people living in Bayanolgy province who saw an Almas. One man (Ravjir) claimed that after an eighteen-month search he saw Almas footprints on the snow on 15 December 1973, and together with two local cattle-breeders followed the tracks for over 11 miles on the first day and 5 miles on the second, before the tracks were lost in the Yolt mountains. On 13 February 1974 Musai, a shepherd, said that he had seen an Almas in the Asgat mountains. The descriptions given were quite consistent, if a little ungrammatical:

. . . half men and half beasts with reddish-black hair. Their face is hairless and their abdomen is sparsely covered with hair. The back of the head has a conical shape as it were, the forehead is flattened, prominent brow ridges and a protruding jaw. The size of a medium-height man, an Almas walks with his knees bent, stoops as is in-toed. He has broad shoulders and long arms; his big toe sticks out. Almases are easily frightened, suspicious, though not aggressive, and lead a nocturnal life. No one has ever heard them speak. They were usually seen at dawn and in the dusk and are believed to live on roots, leaves, grass and other vegetation. They prefer to stay in places far away from man, in mountains for instance. For some unknown reason they keep close to wild rams and goats. In summer, when the cattle are moved from their winter mountain pastures to distant ones their place is taken by the wild rams and goats, and then, as a rule, Almases make their appearance. Cattle breeders once met a couple and once a baby Almas.

This is a fascinating account corroborating much of the earlier material. The correlation between the distribution of Almas and that of the wild sheep and goats could possibly be for reasons of hunting, especially if the account of Almas butchering an ibex (see above) given by the teacher to Ivlov is to be believed.

In 1979 I was able to visit Outer Mongolia and investigate for myself stories about the Almas and their possible connection with Neanderthal man. Before describing the results of my survey, however, we should take a look at reported sightings of Almas and other wildmen elsewhere – in the Caucasus, the Pamir mountains and Siberia.

# Chapter 6
# Reports from the Caucasus

The wildmen of the Caucasus, especially in part of the main range which connects Azerbaijan, Georgia and Daghestan, have been sighted sporadically over the last 100 years and systematically studied for the last twenty. These Caucasian reports describe hominids, communicating with gestures and even, apparently, bartering goods with the local people; they have no place in fairy tale or fable, being thought of as rather a mundane part of the Caucasian fauna. One might reasonably consider them to be a western extension of the Almas of Mongolia, with whom they have many features in common, and whose name I shall adopt to describe them. Alternative names for them include Biaban-guli and Kaptar, the former being quoted in the first account of such a creature produced by a scientist, the zoologist K.A. Satunin, who accidentally encountered a female Biaban-guli in the Talysh hills of the southern Caucasus in 1899.[1] The description of the sighting, which took place at dusk, is rather vague, except for the fact that Professor Satunin was certain that the figure he saw had 'completely human movements'. Nor was he in the mood for phantoms.

My mood before that strange sight had been very prosaic. I had been berating myself mentally for thoughtlessness, my guides for their passion for travelling off the road to the devil knows where, and worrying most of all in case I tore my suede jacket to shreds in pushing through the thickets. And I was in such a sober frame of mind it would be difficult to suggest hallucinations, and besides, the horse and my companions had undoubtedly also seen something. But it was not possible to resolve the question just then. We had just got into such a dense and muddy thicket that we only just managed to get out of it somehow, and arrived at last at the village wearisome of travel.

After a lavish dinner (caviare and chicken pilaf) the good professor listened to his hosts talking about wild people. One man was

inclined to the opinion that wild *men* were no longer to be found in
the Caucasus, nor in Georgia, and only some women remained, one
of which had been the creature encountered *en route*. But others
(clearly those with greater biological acumen) said that both wild
men *and* wild women were still to be found. Various amazing tales
followed, including that of one man who described an encounter
with a really big wildman, very hairy, who left footprints 2 quarters
and 4 fingers long (*c.* $15\frac{3}{4}$ in.). The same hairy man had apparently
been encountered twice more, again in the course of hunting
expeditions, but then the tales and the wildman began to get taller
(doubtless the hour was late). All present, however, concurred that
wild people of some kind lived in the Caucasus and were called
Biaban-guli. Many stories about them appeared later during the
First World War, together with accounts of their characteristic cries.

The second name, Kaptar, was popularized by Yu I. Merezhinski, a senior lecturer at the Department of Ethnography and
Anthropology of Kiev University, who had been working during
the 1950s in the northern Caucasus, in Azerbaijan. A local expert in
night time boar-hunting, Khadzhi Magoma, promised to guide him
to a place where at a certain time of the year the Kaptar was in the
habit of bathing in a stream, if he agreed to take a flash picture of it
and give him one. A small population of albino Kaptars was said to
live near there, and sure enough Merezhinski saw one from a
distance of only a few yards, clearly discernible on the river bank
through the bushes. It was damp, lean and covered from head to
foot with white hair. Unfortunately the reality of the creature was
too much for Merezhinski, who instead of photographing it shot at
it with his revolver but missed in his excitement. The old hunter,
furious at the deception, refused to repeat the experiment.[2]
Merezhinski was not unprepared for the sight since he had come
across mention of such hominids in the course of ethnographic
survey work among the local population. Very recent researchers in
the area, notably John Colarusso, who has worked on the native
languages of the northwest Caucasus, report numerous accounts of
these creatures, described as 'half man and half beast', which live in
thick forests on the mountainsides.[3]

Colarusso accumulated ethnographic evidence about the beliefs
and attitudes of the Caucasians to their wildmen. One of his

informants, Adnan Saygili, spoke of a hunting trip that he and his father had made to the mountains of eastern Turkey, recalling that his father had used the opportunity to familiarize him with the spoor of various animals. He drew on the ground a rough impression which resembled a human footprint, saying that it was the footprint of the 'montane-forest-man' which was not found in Turkey but did live in his native Caucasus. It was not, apparently, dangerous, but might defend itself if a lone hunter blundered into it in thick bush. The footprint was wider than a man's but definitely human.

The Caucasian hunters are apparently quite familiar with the creatures, which are too rare to be a nuisance to farmers and present only the mildest of dangers to the hunters themselves. They are known to be short, around 5 ft tall, covered with brownish hair, to have an ugly protruding face, but to be very agile and strong, walking always upright like a man. Not all are thought to be especially hairy, and they live in the thick forests on mountain slopes and valleys, occasionally coming down to villages to raid cornfields. One of the most interesting assertions, again by Saygili, was that some Caucasian men could gain great esteem by trading with the creatures. Some areas were well known as haunts of the wildman, and the traders would go out there in small parties and camp with their trading goods ('trinkets') on the ground. After a day or two one of the wildmen would appear on the edge of the clearing, concealing one side of his body behind a tree trunk. He always seemed to be the leader of the group, and his appearance was a signal for contact. Simple bartering then took place, the 'trinkets' being exchanged for 'vegetables and things' of little economic importance. The wildmen made use of extensive gestures and tried to imitate the Caucasian dialect spoken by the traders. It would seem, by way of a postscript, that these same wildmen were not averse to trying to attack the traders either on their way up (with trinkets) or down (with vegetables) but that they were not normally aggressive, though very cunning.

Stories about the wildmen are very common throughout the area and terms for the creatures are widespread in the language family. West Circassian, Abkhaz, Abaza and Ubykh each have one term, and East Circassian has two. Universally in the region the terms mean either 'mountain man' or 'montane-forest-man'. Wildman lore seems to be known chiefly to the hunters and farmers of more outlying areas, and is not a constituent of fairy tales. There is a general consensus about his size, appearance and habitat, and an acceptance of him as a hominid. The communication, using gesture supplemented by a struggle to reproduce the sounds of Circassian, is especially interesting in view of what will be said in Chapter 9 about Neanderthal man's reduced speech capacity. Circassian and its sister tongues are reported to be extraordinarily complex (West Circassian has 68 consonants and Ubykh 81), so it is scarcely surprising that it might be a little difficult to learn.

There seems to be a clear distinction in the minds of Caucasians between the wildmen, whom they regard as merely an un-remarkable component of the local fauna, and the occasional hairy giant who occurs in fables. However, there *are* occasional sightings of larger creatures, just to complicate matters, and a story of two visiting Russians who saw giants 10 ft tall in 1967.[4] This might be dismissed as the result of an excess of vodka, but the sightings did take place very high in the mountain snowfields, in broad daylight. It is not impossible that the creatures were Yetis of the kind clearly living downrange in the Pamirs (Chapter 7), as their habitat is quite wrong for the small manlike Caucasian Almas under discussion.

There is one very famous example of a captured Almas from the Caucasus – the female nicknamed Zana, who lived and was 'domesticated' in the village of Tkhina on the Mokvi river. The human population of the Caucasus is renowned for its longevity, and Porshnev himself was able to obtain eye-witness descriptions from people who, as small children, had been present at Zana's burial in the 1880s. It would seem that she had been captured in the forests of Mt Zaadan and kept at first in a stone enclosure. After three years like this she graduated to a wooden cage, then a house. Her skin was a greyish-black colour, covered with reddish hair, longer on her head than elsewhere. She was capable of inarticulate cries but never developed a language. She had a large face with big cheek bones, muzzle-like prognathous jaw and large eyebrows, big white teeth and a 'fierce expression'. Apparently able to run as fast as a horse, she eventually began to defend herself against the guard dogs with a branch, and learnt to manipulate stones, bashing one against the other. Significantly, the Russian Professor A.A. Mas-hkovtsev later found a Neanderthal-style flint point on the hill where Zana had lived – but we do not know whether Zana had made it herself. Virtually a slave, she learnt to obey simple orders given either by voice or gesture and would, apparently, eat anything that was offered to her, being especially fond of meat. Eventually she became pregnant by one of her human captors, but her first infant died, although in four subsequent pregnancies she produced two sons and two daughters, whose descendants still live in the village.

In 1964 Porshnev visited two of Zana's grandchildren in the town of Tkvartcheli where they worked in a mine. Many of the local people could remember their parents and produce detailed descriptions, mentioning powerful bodies with rather dark skin, totally human. The youngest son, Khvit, died aged between sixty-five and seventy, and apparently had curly hair, prominent lips and a relatively small head and body. He also had a strong and powerful voice, married twice and left three children. The daughter, Gamassa, was reportedly twice as strong as an average female, with a dark, hairy skin. She, too, lived into her sixties. The grandchildren, Chalikoua and Taia, had darkish skin of rather negroid appearance, with very prominent chewing muscles and extra strong jaws. They were also endowed with the curious ability to mimic all animal voices. Zana's tomb was apparently opened in 1965, but there are grounds for doubting that the excavation was in the right place, so we are denied an accurate anthropological report on her skeleton. But we do have the eye-witnesses, and her living descendants. If Zana was a hominid as is suggested, then she belonged to a species that would interbreed with modern man, meaning that she was a member of the *Homo sapiens* family, the only known representative of which, other than ourselves, is Neanderthal man (*Homo sapiens neanderthalensis*). At the time everyone believed her to be an Almas, and had there been any question of her being a feral child someone, surely, would have commented. So the links between Almas and Neanderthal man in this instance seem quite strong.

The story of Zana is only the tip of an iceberg. A number of distinguished Soviet scientists have worked on this problem in the

Caucasus, beginning in 1959–60 with an expedition involving Merezhinski (above), Professor A.A. Mashkovtsev and S.M. Lukomskii, but the person most closely associated with the research is Dr Zh. I. Kofman, a doctor, anatomist and mountaineer who has undertaken fieldwork in the region from 1960 onwards. Dr Kofman (whose first name is frequently given as Marie-Jeanne and whose surname is misspelt Koffman in western literature) was a successor of Boris Porshnev, and actually born in France, although she returned to Russia in 1935. As well as having a brilliant medical career, she became a celebrated climber, and took part in the 1958 Pamir expedition (Chapter 7). She commanded a battalion of alpine troops during the war and received several Soviet military decorations. No one could suggest that the results of her work on the Almas would be other than totally reliable.[5] Her initial studies were conducted in northern Azerbaijan and later concentrated in the Kabardino-Balkaria area. Relatively little has been published.[6] Her early work applied modern polling techniques to the local inhabitants to build 'identikit' Almas, in which she firmly believes and publicly states to be relict Neanderthals. Thirty per cent of the interviews which she carried out she rejected as unreliable, and the remainder produced a convincing portrait gathered from people of very different backgrounds over a wide area. She announced her findings to the Russian Geographical Society in Moscow in March 1966, giving the following description: 'The brow low, narrow and backward-sloping, the nose small and flat as if pinched back, the receding chin round and heavy, and the cheek bones high and Mongolian in character.' Her words were accompanied by a drawing produced from the descriptions – which was a very typical Neanderthal.

The survey also produced two sites where Almas had heaped up stores of vegetable foods, and at the village of Batekh, Zolsk region, a sighting of an Almas girl who had been separately reported by thirty different witnesses. The girl had apparently been searching a maize field for the sweetest corn cobs and had left tooth impressions on the ones she discarded.

Dr Kofman is still continuing her work in the north Caucasus, where all the reported hominids are man-size. In 1978 reports came out that she had found and photographed a set of good tracks and made plaster casts. These have not yet been published, although a young anatomist colleague, Andrei Kozlov, has now started research into Almas anatomy as revealed by their tracks. The very latest sighting from the area of Kofman's search, but collected by Aleksandra Burtseva,[7] tells of two local teenagers mowing grass in July 1980 in an open space some 500 yards from the Nalchik-Pyatigorsk highway. Raised above the ground there is an open water duct running across the field in which the boys took dips from time to time. At one moment they looked in the direction of the duct and saw a hairy creature, not much taller than themselves, standing on the edge of the duct looking at them. The boys stood motionless and surprised while the creature entertained them with all sorts of antics: running with great speed to and fro on the edge of the duct, jumping from it, somersaulting, etc. (not unlike the playful Almas from Mongolia). The boys had the impression that the creature was inviting them to take part, but they were frightened and, after a while, obviously disappointed, the Almas left and disappeared in a hemp field nearby. The boys went home and recounted their tale to unsurprised mothers who agreed that it must have been a young Almas. The incident happened at noon and in full view of the Nalchik-Pyatigorsk highway, often travelled by tourists from all over Europe and sometimes from America.

Other recent sightings have taken place at the Chegem river. In May and September 1979 a man and his brother, out to cut wood, saw a manlike creature at a distance of about 60 ft. It was about the same height as they and covered in dark hair, with long hair on the head, heavy shoulders, thin arms, long hands with long fingers and nails. The skin was brown and the palms of the hands were hairless. They particularly noted that the forehead overhung the eyes like a peaked cap, and that the eyes themselves were slanted and the nose aquiline.[8] This all sounds very Neanderthaloid (Chapter 9). The September sighting took place in the same spot about noon, and this time the hominid was nearer, clearly visible lying in the grass on his right side about 30 ft away. His back was entirely covered with hair except for the buttocks, and his skin was brown. One of the human spectators tried to approach him, but he sat up, turned and ran away.

With Dr Kofman working in the north and Professor N.I.

Burchak-Abramovitch in southern Azerbaijan, the Caucasian reconnaissance is becoming very systematic. Dr Kofman has taken full details of all encounters, including the precise time of day, date, etc. and the sex of the Almas concerned. Significantly, few juveniles like the one seen near the Nalchik-Pyatigorsk highway have been observed in the Caucasus, and more males than females. This exhaustive twenty-year survey, made by travelling on foot or on horseback for several months of the year between villages, has resulted in the accumulation of an immense treasure-house of information, at least as good as that of Zhamtsarano and probably just as inaccessible. If it were ever fully published in the West it might settle once and for all the question of the authenticity of Almas-sightings in the Caucasus. In the meantime I am prepared to believe that the ethnographic and eye-witness evidence is already sufficient proof of the existence of a manlike creature with pronounced Neanderthal characteristics in this region.

# Chapter 7
# The
# Pamir Expeditions

Although Tibet is often referred to as 'the roof of the world' the name could be applied more correctly to the even higher mountain ranges comprising the Pamirs, which form a complex knot of high mountains, glaciers, ice fields and alpine meadows lying between Soviet Central Asia, Sinkiang, Kashmir and Afghanistan. Most of the Pamirs are, in fact, in Soviet territory, but almost their sole inhabitants are the nomadic Tajik tribes, together with the occasional party of explorers, mountaineers or prospectors. The word 'pamir' means a mountain valley of glacial origin and the valleys themselves, generally at altitudes of 12,000–14,000 ft, often contain streams which may feed a series of lakes, and include patches of alpine meadow (in the short summer when the area is not completely snow-covered) which produce excellent pasturage for animals. The valleys suffer, however, from an almost total lack of timber and ground suitable for cultivation. The Pamirs consist of a series of eight separate ranges, each crowned by peaks over 20,000 ft, seamed with ice fields and terminating in glacial moraines. They are often described as savage, inhospitable and desolate, and are certainly very remote; as late as 1926 a scientific expedition found a village there which had had no contact with the outside world for centuries and had developed quite separately.[1]

From the hominid point of view the area clearly has great potential as a refuge, and evidence suggests that it conceals both the small Almas-like variety and the larger, Yeti-type, primate. Recent Soviet work by teams of dedicated amateurs has generated considerable public interest and produced new and dramatic sightings, footprints and 'contacts'. The story really starts, however, in 1925, when Major-General Mikhail Stephanovitch Top-ilski, Commissar of a mounted regiment, was pursuing White Russian forces as they retreated. He later recalled:[2]

Continuing our chase, we caught up with what was left of the
exhausted gang, who had stopped for a rest at a place where the
glacier was split apart by a stone cliff. The upper tongue of the
glacier hung from the cliff in which there was a crevice or cave. We
surrounded the gang and took up a position above where they were
resting. A machine-gun was placed in position. When we threw the
first grenade, a man (a Russian officer) ran out onto the glacier and
started shouting that the shooting would make the ice cave in and
that everyone would be buried. When we demanded that they
surrender he asked for time to talk it over with the other bandits,
and went back into the cave. Soon after we heard an ominous
hissing as the ice began to move. At almost the same moment we
heard shots, and not knowing what they meant decided that it was
the beginning of an assault.

Pieces of snow and ice started falling down from the cliff,
gradually burying the entrance to the cave. When it was nearly
buried three men managed to escape, and the rest (we learned later
that there were five) were buried under the debris. Our shots killed
two of the bandits and seriously wounded the third. When we
reached him, he showed us the spot where the body of a Russian
officer was buried and we dug it out. The wounded man turned out
to be an Uzbek tea-house owner from Samarkand.

We questioned him and he gave us the following information.
While the bandits were discussing our order to surrender, some
hairy man-like creatures, howling inarticulately, appeared in the
cave through a crevice (which possibly led upwards from the cave).
There were several of them, and they had sticks in their hands. The
bandits tried to shoot their way through. One of the bandits was
killed by the creatures with sticks. Our narrator received a blow
from a stick on his shoulder, and rushed to the cave entrance with
one of the monsters hard on his heels. It ran out of the cave after
him, but he shot it and it was buried under the snow.

To check up on this strange story we made him show us the exact
spot and cleared the snow away. We recovered the body all right. It
had three bullet wounds. Not far off we found a stick made of very
hard wood, though it cannot be stated for certain that it belonged to
the creature. At first glance I thought the body was that of an ape. It
was covered with hair all over. But I knew there were no apes in the
Pamirs. Also, the body itself looked very much like that of a man.
We tried pulling the hair, to see if it was just a hide used for disguise,
but found that it was the creature's own natural hair. We turned the
body over several times on its back and its front, and measured it.
Our doctor (who was killed later the same year) made a long and
thorough inspection of the body, and it was clear that it was not a
human being.

The body belonged to a male creature 165–170 cm [5 ft 5 in.–5 ft 7
in.] tall, elderly or even old, judging by the greyish colour of the hair
in several places. The chest was covered with brownish hair and the

belly with greyish hair. The hair was longer but sparser on the chest and close-cropped and thick on the belly. In general the hair was very thick, without any underfur. There was least hair on the buttocks, from which fact our doctor deduced that the creature sat like a human being. There was most hair on the hips. The knees were completely bare of hair and had callous growths on them. The whole foot including the sole was quite hairless and was covered by hard brown skin. The hair got thinner near the hand, and the palms had none at all but only callous skin.

The colour of the face was dark, and the creature had neither beard nor moustache. The temples were bald and the back of the head was covered by thick, matted hair. The dead creature lay with its eyes open and its teeth bared. The eyes were dark and the teeth were large and even and shaped like human teeth. The forehead was slanting and the eyebrows were very powerful. The protruding jawbones made the face resemble the Mongol type of face. The nose was flat, with a deeply sunk bridge. The ears were hairless and looked a little more pointed than a human being's with a longer lobe. The lower jaw was very massive.

The creature had a very powerful chest and well developed muscles. We didn't find any important anatomical difference between it and man. The genitalia were like man's. The arms were of normal length, the hands were slightly wider and the feet much wider and shorter than man's.

The creature's close resemblance to a man clearly disconcerted the troops who, unable to take the body with them for further examination, buried it ceremonially under a cairn of stones, in much the same way, one is tempted to think, that their forebears gave funerals to Neanderthal dead some 40,000 years before.

Topilski first revealed his story to the Leningrad hydrologist, A.G. Pronin, whose own sightings in this area add another important contribution to the saga.[3] Aleksandr Georgievitch Pronin is a Senior Researcher in the Geographical Research Institute, Leningrad University, and in 1957 was heading a hydrological team attached to a big scientific expedition on the edge of the Fedchenko glacier. This huge glacier complex, previously quite unknown, has only just been surveyed from the air by Uzbek scientists, but at the time Pronin was writing even the altitude and positions of the major peaks had not been determined. On 2 August 1957 the team camped on the fringe of the glacier and some of his colleagues went off on horseback to the nearest village for supplies. Pronin himself was investigating the valley of the Balyandkiik river and at noon he noticed a figure standing on a rocky cliff about 500 yards above him and the same distance away. His first reaction was surprise, since this area was known to be uninhabited, and his second that the creature was not human. It resembled a man but was very stooped. He watched the stocky figure move across the snow, keeping its feet wide apart, and he noted that its forearms were longer than a human's and it was covered with reddish grey hair. After about five minutes it disappeared behind a rock, but three days later when Pronin was returning from a reconnaissance expedition he saw it again in the same valley. This time it was later, about sunset, and again the figure was walking upright, but it quickly disappeared into a black hollow, possibly a cave.

Pronin was modestly most reluctant to come to any conclusion about the creature's nature since he considered himself not competent to judge anything except hydrological matters. At first it seems he thought it was a bear, but then concluded it was definitely manlike. The story has a curious postscript. A week or so later the members of the expedition found that their inflatable rubber boat had gone missing from its position on the river bank, and they hunted for it to no avail, very puzzled since this was an uninhabited area. Although Pronin did not know it at the time, the boat was eventually found by his colleagues 3 miles higher up the river, which at that point was full of cataracts and waterfalls. It is very difficult (not to say impossible) to suggest how it might have got there unless someone had carried it.

Pronin told his story to the Snowman Commission at the invitation of the Praesidium of the Soviet Academy of Sciences. The local Kirghiz mountain people were apparently quite familiar with these creatures, which are called *Guli-avan* (or *Golub-yavan*) in the region, which just means 'wildman', and some reported the loss of various household articles which were often found some distance away in the mountains. The area is so remote that it could shelter, in its deep caves, a veritable army of Almas, living as omnivores on small rodents, edible berries and plants such as sea buckthorn and sweetbriar. Perhaps significantly, the very same page of *Soviet Weekly* (15 January 1958) which contained Pronin's account had, in the corner, a brief mention of new Neanderthal sites in Uzbekistan with finds including paintings and mineral pigments. The distance between the regions is no more than a few hundred miles. Neanderthals were certainly around in this area 50,000 years ago, and the question remains whether either Topilski or Pronin saw their descendants.

The interest of the Academy of Sciences in this whole question was not confined to the establishment of a Commission, and in 1958 an expedition to the Pamirs was organized with the dual purpose of collecting primary data on these Snowmen, and other scientific information as well. The leader was a botanist, Professor K.V. Stanyukovitch, and the personnel including not only Professor Porshnev but Dr Kofman, later to do so much work on this matter in the Caucasus. Stanyukovitch seems to have been rather more keen on working on his botanical atlas than devoting much attention to the Snowman problem, and Porshnev later complained that he was sent to the wrong place, and that the expedition did not really study the Snowman problem at all, but concentrated on the biogeography and history of the Pamirs in general.[4] Furthermore, Porshnev ridiculed the fact that the team did not include a primatologist, anthropologist or mammalogist, and systematic field diaries were not kept. No proper scientific accounts were published, two relatively short references being all that was produced.[5] This is almost unbelievable, since the expedition lasted nine months and was equipped with concealed observation posts, telescopic lenses and sheepdogs 'trained' by Moscow Zoo to follow the trail of large apes. More than twenty sheep and goats were used as bait, and nets and snares were laid for the unfortunate Snowmen in more than thirty places. They evaded both these and experienced snow-leopard hunters,[6] and the expedition returned empty-handed, which was a sad blow for the Snowman Commission and represents about the last example of official funding for such research in the USSR. All the recent work has been carried out by amateurs and has, significantly, produced more information.

Stanyukovitch's main claim to fame seems to be the writing in 1958 of a science fiction story about the creatures, called 'The man who saw it'.[7] This was the story of a lone researcher who was tracking the last Abominable Snowman on earth somewhere in the Pamirs. The tracker has an overwhelming advantage: a rucksack. He has a stock of provisions, while his quarry, a pitiable creature, must stop to gather food. The story ends with both of them falling into a raging river. The man finally swims to the shore, but the Snowman drowns.

The work of recent Soviet amateur expeditions has caused a great furore in Snowman circles. Operating at lower altitudes in the Pamir range, they have found large, not Almas-size, creatures. Two issues of *Komsomol'skaya Pravda* (the paper of the Russian youth movement) in 1979 (15 August and 8 September) reported an expedition from Kiev, working at the end of the summer in the Gissar (Pamir) range, which described its findings with the aid of Igor' Burtsev, a long-time worker in the Snowman field who is attached to the Darwin Museum at Moscow. The expedition was led by Igor' Tatsl, a worker in the 'Bolshevik' factory in Kiev who, in company with friends, spends his annual holidays in this area looking for hominids. In 1979 the area chosen was one of the ravines at the headwaters of the Varzob river, and on 4 August the expedition pitched camp at the confluence of two rivers and began night observations with special viewing equipment and day investigations of the slopes of nearby ravines for footprints. They smoothed and prepared special 'footprint zones' in the few suitable spots, although much of the ground was hard and stony and covered with gravel. Some of the tracks which subsequently appeared could have been left by bare feet, but it was often difficult to judge the size – a heel print might occur where the toes had been stepping on stones, for example. One thing which did emerge was a marked correlation between the appearance of tracks and the nights when no watches were being set, so the expedition restricted itself to night watches from the tents instead of using hides. On the morning of 15 August four clear prints made by bare feet were observed, two leading towards the camp and two away from it. Pace length was 3 ft 10 in., twice that of the average human pace, and the tracks were some 50 yards from the tent. However, none was suitable for obtaining a good, deep impression.

Interest was also taken in the views of the local people, including a forestry worker (Kul'beddin Radzhabov) who directed the inquirers to the house of a huntsman (Gafar Dzhabirov) with an interesting story to tell. He reported having seen – and taken a shot at – one of the creatures in the mid-1960s when he had visited a ravine 3.75 miles from the village of Khakimi to mow the cane. After finishing the mowing he felt uneasy and turning saw, some 15 yards away, a 'sort of wild hairy man, almost black in colour', sitting on a large rock and looking at him. Gafar took fright, grabbed his gun and took a shot at it, but when he opened his eyes the creature had gone.

On 21 August 1979, after most of the team had gone out to continue explorations, one of the members found a huge clear footprint in powdery black soil. Another one, not so clear, was located some short distance away. The print length was $13\frac{1}{2}$ in. and the breadth at the toes $6\frac{1}{4}$ in. (very comparable with the Himalayan examples). The big toe was significantly larger than the others and the toes slightly spread. The foot was also remarkably flat. Lacquer was used to harden the soil before a plaster cast was taken. The print bore striking resemblances to some of the American Bigfoot ones, but since Burtsev himself was the only one who knew what these looked like the possibility of a fake seems very small. Unfortunately the expedition was scheduled to leave the area two days after this discovery, although it returned the following year.

An expedition mounted in 1980 was much larger than the one the year before, comprising nearly 120 people. Two sightings were made and reported, one of which was picked up by British newspapers. *The Times* (2 June 1981) printed the story of one member of the expedition, eighteen-year-old Nina Grineva, under the headline 'Yeti described as huge, hairy and shy'; a more substantial version of the same story, entitled 'The day she said hello to a Yeti', appeared in the *Sunday Express* (31 May 1981). Neither account is particularly accurate, and one has to turn to the Russian report for a full version. Nina Grineva is quoted there as follows:[8]

He was standing some 25 meters away, facing me and piercing my very soul with his glance. It was not aggressive, rather well wishing, but piercing. The eyes were big and glowing. They were not bright but glowing. And all his body was sort of glowing. He was dark and at the same time somewhat silvery. I could see his body was covered with hair, but it was not shaggy. Maybe it was wet, anyhow the colour had a silvery tint. He was about two meters tall. His figure looked very hefty, square and straight from shoulder to hip, with a short neck, the head put forward, the arms hanging down freely in a somewhat forward position too. When I saw him I was not scared and began slowly to advance to him. Having gone about five steps, I held out and pressed two or three times a rubber toy in the shape of a bird, which made a squeaking sound and was given to me by Tatsl [her companion] in order to attract *Gosha's attention with its sound. But it was this that spoiled our contact. Gosha made a sharp turn and quickly went down the slope to the river and disappeared beyond the steep bank. I noted the softness and grace of his walk, though he moved very fast. It was not a human walk but as of an animal, as of a panther. Despite boulders and other obstacles, he moved quickly, softly and even gracefully. He must have a perfect sense of balance and to him a steep and uneven slope is like a paved road for us. I was much disappointed by his retreat. But nothing could be done. I turned around and started to walk in the opposite direction, towards the crossing. At that point my memory faded and I don't remember what I did. No, I was not frightened. On the contrary, I regretted very much that he had gone. But I sort of passed out. I don't know how I reached the water and what I did there. I came to when Zhora was shaking me. Then I showed her where I had seen HIM.[11]

* Her name for the creature.

In a comment made in August 1981, Dmitri Bayanov of the Darwin Museum described 'two rather tense sessions of the [hominid problem] seminar devoted to the event'.[9] Although participants in the expedition faced a very critical audience, on balance Bayanov believes in the report despite strong disapproval of the way in which the contact was made. Bayanov considers that the girl was used as bait, which may be good copy for humorists, but could end in tragedy. Members of Tatsl's own group suggested that he and Nina broke the basic rules of mountain climbing, which left her alone in a dangerous situation. One very interesting thing is that both she and some of the others had heard sounds of stone-bashing away from the base camp before the creature's appearance – a characteristic noise also made, it seems, by Bigfoot.

A 1981 expedition to the Pamirs consisted of 160 members from all over the USSR. Several sightings were reported[10] but no clear descriptions. However, a footprint was found on 29 September by Vadim Makarov which is not only the biggest yet ($19\frac{1}{4}$ in.) but has four toes. Such aberrant varieties have been reported both from the Himalayas and from America, and are generally thought to be deformities. The prints were found on the bank of the same river

23 *The famous four-toed Yeti footprint found by Vadim Makarov on 29 September 1981 in the Pamir mountains. It is* $19\frac{1}{4}$ *in. long.*

where the Grineva encounter had taken place the previous year, and equal in size the huge prints now found in China. There can be little doubt of the existence of a large apelike creature in the Pamirs, although at present one can go no further than that.

Publication of these finds is restricted, so far, to Russian newspapers and periodicals dealing with current affairs, for example, the 'Inquirers' Club' of the youth-movement paper *Komsomol'skaya Pravda* or the multi-language weekly magazine *Moscow News*. Friends at the Darwin Museum (Moscow) tell me that their work has generated a vast amount of public interest but, as yet, no official government sponsorship. No doubt the Academy of Sciences is not anxious to repeat the Stanyukovitch failure of 1958 – but the recent Chinese work with official backing might engender a useful spirit of competition.

Despite the fact that the early sightings (Pronin and Topilski) took place in a slightly different area it is perhaps surprising that no Almas-like creatures have been spotted by recent expeditions. Either their distribution is restricted to one locality or they no longer exist, a fate which may also be in store for the Mongolian Almas. Descriptions of the two varieties in the Pamirs have little in common; the reports seem to describe two separate creatures, of which only one (the Almas) can be considered a hominid. Descriptions of the larger type appear to fit well within the range for the Yeti (in the Himalayas) or related creatures reported from China and Siberia. The smaller type fits in equally well with descriptions of Almas from Mongolia, Tien Shan and the Caucasus, all of which are geographically-related areas linked by mountain chains. It would be good to think that in the Pamirs we have an example of co-existence between two varieties of unclassified primate, but until their distribution can be shown to overlap such an attractive hypothesis cannot be proved.

# Chapter 8
# Siberian Snowmen

Some of the most interesting of the Russian wildmen reports come from Siberia: two types of wildmen are recorded, one extremely manlike and the other a larger variety (which bears a distinct resemblance to the Yeti), complete with appropriate folktales and local legends. The former seems to be confined to an area northeast of Yakut in eastern Siberia, while the latter has been observed sporadically right across Siberia, from the Urals in the west to the Chukot peninsula of the extreme east. This is a truly enormous range, perhaps 5,000 miles at its maximum extent, yet here again we see a remarkable similarity between many of the descriptions, although it would also be true to say that these hairy denizens of the tundra and coniferous forests have inspired their fair share of 'tall' stories.

It is almost impossible to envisage the bleakness and remoteness of Siberia, an area of over 5 million square miles. Population densities are low, despite the new Soviet attempts at colonization over the last twenty years, and the people who live here tend to be semi-nomadic reindeer herders. A large proportion of the sightings and stories come from these people, with the balance made up of reports from visiting scientists or academics who have occasionally interested themselves in these matters and collated some of the local accounts. One such person was the geologist Vladimir Pushkarev, who produced an article in 1978 containing typical stories from the area.[1] Some of these are very circumstantial and highly believable, for example the detailed account quoted below, told to Pushkarev by a Russian veteran living in the village of Ust-Tsil'm in the area of the lower Pechora river (just to the west of the northern Ural mountains). The sighting took place in 1920 when the man, then aged about fifteen, was mowing hay by the Tsil'm river some 6 miles from his village. Such a scene should already be familiar to readers, since we have come across at least half a dozen similar encounters where people were working outside their villages, chopping wood, mowing hay, etc., and a surprising number of these incidents took place near rivers. Here is the Russian veteran's story:

I along with six boys and two adults was stacking the hay 300 m from the river. A hut in which we lived during haymaking stood not far away. Suddenly on the opposite bank two incomprehensible figures appeared. One was small and black, the other of immense height (over 2 m), grey, whitish. They were like people in every way but we felt at once that these weren't people, and looked at them without moving. They began to run around a large willow. The whitish one ran off and the black one chased after him. It was as if they were playing. They ran very quickly. We didn't notice any clothing on them. This went on for several minutes, then they darted towards the river and disappeared. We ran right away to the hut and didn't dare come out for a whole hour. Then, having armed ourselves with whatever came to hand and grabbed a gun, we rowed in a boat to where they had been running. There we found both large and small tracks. They were particularly numerous round the willow. I don't remember toes on the prints of the small one, but I inspected the tracks of the big one properly. They were very large, as if made by winter boots. The toes were sharply defined. There were six of them, approximately equal in length. The print was very similar to a human one, but flat like a bear's, and the toes weren't pressed together as a man's would be, but spread a little outwards.

This is an interesting account for two reasons, firstly because so many people had seen the creatures (and corroborative accounts were obtained from other villagers) and secondly because of the sighting of a large and small wildman together. Inevitably one must ask whether the small one was an infant of the same species. It would be wrong to put too much emphasis on detailed descriptions of footprints written down after fifty years, but from these and from the apparent size of the 'adult' the sighting could have been of Yeti-like creatures.

A comparable sighting from the same general area (near the Ai-yu-va river in the Komi ASSR, just west of the Urals) was reported by a certain Mr and Mrs Kharalampov, who were travelling in this district as tourists in 1956 and came across some unusual creatures, tall, manlike, 'magnificently built', without clothing and covered in long black hair. A ringing 'inhuman' call was also mentioned, and the creatures had been observed swimming in the river before emerging and setting up a clamour on the other side. Again, the report has come from people who were presumably unaffected by (and indeed ignorant of) local folktales and can have had no vested interest in disseminating them. Two further interesting features are, of course, the high-pitched call, so characteristic of the Yeti, and the association with water, commonly reported also for the Sasquatch. This latter is a particularly frequent theme in Siberia, where a large number of wildmen have been observed actually swimming or wading across the rivers, although, of course, similar occurrences have been reported from elsewhere. It is most difficult to account for, since the Siberian rivers remain frozen for most of the year, which places most of the sightings in the summer months. Of course, the northern plains of Siberia are covered with rivers and it is impossible to travel anywhere without crossing them. Presumably there are certain favoured crossing points, used by both locals and wildmen, which would account for the sightings.

The redoubtable Pushkarev also travelled in the extensive drainage system of the Ob' river, on the other (eastern) side of the Ural range from the Pechora, and again recorded some good wildman sightings. In August 1975 he was in the Vasyakova region, accompanied by one Viktoriya Pupko from the Moscow Institute of Civil Engineering, and was introduced by the chairman of the city council to a man named Luka Vasil'evitch Tynzyanov, who recounted the following story:

In 1960 or 1961 I was going one evening from Yaraskogort to Vasyakovo along the bank of the Mountain Ob. I had two dogs with me. They suddenly bared their teeth, began to bark and rushed forward. Then they returned, then ran ahead again and again returned. They pressed themselves against me in fear and stopped barking. Just then two hulking creatures came out of the forest. One was tall, more than two metres, the other a little less. I too took fright because their eyes burnt dark-red like two lanterns. They came to meet me and on drawing level suddenly looked at me with those glowing eyes. They had no clothes at all; they had a thick coat of short hair on their bodies. Both head and body were all black. The face projected forwards, the arms were rather long, longer than a man's, and they swung their arms in rather a strange manner. Their gait was somewhat unusual, not human. They turned their legs out a little in walking. When the monsters had gone past, the dogs at once bolted for the village.

Leaving aside the use of the word 'monsters', the account does agree rather well with the other stories given so far in this chapter. The mention that the creature frightened the dogs is a recurring theme in these Siberian stories. The man who told this particular tale gave the creatures' local name as *Uten-ekhti-agen* ('the one who wanders in the forests') and said that he had seen them on four separate occasions, the last two being less than fifteen years ago.

Similar stories are very widespread on the lower Ob' river and around the delta of the rivers Synya and Voikar. There is an element of local superstition, since some people were unwilling to tell the stories, either because they felt that sighting the creature brought bad luck, or because since its existence was not officially recognized such a description might meet with official disapproval. This remote area is a long way from Moscow and its inhabitants, Khantys (Ostyaks), are rather trusting and credulous. Pushkarev mentions, and I feel that this is significant, that most of the stories of wildmen were not told to him by professional local story-tellers who might be expected to know them, but by the local fishermen and reindeer herders who did not know any other historic tales and seemed to have no reason to invent them. Better-educated people also revealed stories, notably Marfa Efimovna Sen'kina, formerly a village schoolmistress and the widow of the renowned revolutionary who established Soviet power in the Ob' area:

Before the Revolution my father and I constantly travelled on business all over the Ob' area of the north and the Yamal peninsula. I was then twenty, and we were based in Salckhard. We often stayed with a certain old Ostyak not far from the settlement of Puiko. I remember September had just begun, the nights were already dark, and our dogs often barked during the night. Once the barking became especially ferocious. This happened two nights in succession. I asked our Ostyak hosts what they were barking at, and he answered in a whisper that the Surveyor was coming. 'What sort of Surveyor is this', I asked, not understanding. 'I'll show you tonight', he promised, 'but only look at him with care – through your fingers'. At midnight we left the tent. The moon was already out, large and red. We waited, probably, for about an hour. Suddenly against the barking of the dogs, several tens of metres away I saw an unusually tall man. A two-metre purple willow surrounded our tents. The man was head and shoulders above it. He strode very quickly and surely straight through the brushwood. His eyes glowed like two lanterns. I had never met so strange and tall a man.

The dogs, barking, sprang at him. One, excited by our presence, ran right up to him. The man bent down and seizing it threw it far to one side. We heard only a short squeal and the body flashing through the air. The man went swiftly off, not turning once. 'What was that, a *leskii* [wood-goblin]?' I asked the old man. 'Don't say that word', he said, frightened. 'You'll summon him. Just call him the Surveyor. He comes here every year at this time.' Apparently dozens of people had seen at various times this strange forest creature.

Again, the story has been produced by someone whose word we have no reason to doubt. The general description of the creature, including its height and the glowing eyes, matches other accounts, as does its unhappy effect on the dogs.

I cannot resist giving yet one further example, this time a very famous 19th-century sighting (the so-called Berezovo wonder) which sparked off what must be the strangest-ever criminal case, whose documents are preserved in the archives of the local museum. Two trappers, Falalei Lykysov (an Ostyak) and Obyl' (a Samoyed), killed a 'monster' in the forests of the Berezovo region in 1845. The creature was described as being of human build and about 3 arshins (7 ft) tall, but unfortunately had other less realistic attributes including one eye on its forehead and one on its cheek. A retired Tsarist village policeman sent a report of this event to the Berezovo district council on 16 December 1845, and it is also mentioned in the annual of the Tobol'sk provincial museum at the later date of 1907. The trappers had apparently come upon the creature in the forest where it was being attacked (yet again) by their dogs, and defending itself with its hands. Falalei fired at it from a distance of about 35 yards and it toppled to the ground. The trappers were then able to make a close inspection and noted the thick coat of blackish hair which covered it all over (Siberian 'Yetis' seem to have blackish hair, rather than the reddish hair found on their southerly relatives). The creature was a male, with rather pointed heels and no toes on its feet, claw-like fingers, and flesh of rather a blackish colour. In many ways this description would seem to fit a bear more than a man, but one must presume that the trappers were familiar with bears and the rest of the local fauna, so that there should be no question of a mistake. The resulting police case came about because the locals refused to show the district police officer where they had left the body after he had found out about the incident, resulting in an unsolved murder which remains on an open file. Had it not been for the involvement of the police one would be tempted to dismiss the whole thing as a fabrication, yet surely no policeman makes an official report of a shooting of some strange creature unless he feels that someone has done something wrong, or at least that the matter should be investigated. The inference is that the trappers were uncertain exactly what they had shot, since it did not conform to anything they had seen before, and they admitted to themselves that it might have been manlike (thus meaning that they had committed murder), which explains their refusal to show the police where they had left the body. All the same, it is an enigma.

A survey was tried on the pupils of the three vocational secondary schools in the town of Salekhard, near the mouth of the Ob' river, where children from the whole of the Yamalo-Nenets national region are taught. These children are the offspring of nomadic reindeer herders and are trained to be teachers, medical assistants and livestock experts. Sixty pupils were questioned, of whom forty-eight admitted that either they or a relative had or had not seen a wildman on the tundra, and the remaining twelve answered 'don't know'. To the next question – what name did the Nentsy (Samoyeds) give to the creature? – all sixty pupils answered *'tungu'*. A third question, asking whether the child personally or any close relatives had seen the creature recently (in the 1960s or 1970s), met with a more varied response. Four said that they had seen a *tungu* with their own eyes, but at some distance and in deep twilight, and could not give a detailed description. Ten reported that their father, grandfather or brothers had seen one. Asked to describe the creature, four children said that it was very tall and thin, hairy, and able to run very fast. They also mentioned a cry like a 'deafening whistle'. Locations of sightings were all over the northern plain of western Siberia, from the Ob' to the Yenisei, on the tundra of the Gydan peninsula, and further south in the forests round the Nadym and Taz rivers.

A continuation of the survey among the adult fishermen and reindeer breeders of the hamlet of Nyda in Nadym district showed total agreement that such a creature existed. However, they all insisted that although the *tungu* had been encountered quite frequently up to fifteen to twenty years ago, for about the past ten years it had not been met at all. Some thought that it might have retreated into the forests further south, perhaps as a result of increasing geological and constructional surveys in the area. The Nentsy (Samoyeds) never, it seems, confuse the modern people called Tungus with the wild *tungus*, and consequently produce very precise and standardized descriptions.

Most sightings seem to have taken place in the autumn, when the tundra is plunged into a kind of twilight for much of the time. The *tungus* are always described as very tall (about 6 ft 6 in.), which may not seem excessively tall to us but both Tungus and Samoyeds are rather short races. The *tungus* live in the coniferous forests, supposedly beneath projecting tree roots (a belief which finds an echo in medieval wildman legends) and cannot speak, although they can whistle, make inarticulate cries and call something like 'ru-ru-ru-'. In 1962 one *tungu* threw sand into the tent of a herdsman and made his characteristic cry – but no one went out, as they were afraid. The herdsman in question, Evgenii Grigor'evich Tog, had seen *tungu* tracks before, in 1929, and described them as being rather long and narrow.

One might draw the general conclusion from the foregoing discussion that there is a *prima facie* case for the existence of a Yeti-type primate (*tungu*) in western Siberia which differs a little from Himalayan and Chinese examples in hair colour and predilection for water, and which seems to live in the coniferous forest areas to the south of the tundra in the many river systems that cross Siberia. Many of the sightings reported by reindeer herders and fishermen appear to be authentic, but there is undoubtedly a gloss of folktale. However, on balance, the sheer persistence of very similar accounts over such a vast space must mean that there is a case to answer.

The stories about a tall Yeti-like creature also extend to the extreme east of Russia. Aleksandra Burtseva, an engineer, recently summarized some interesting accounts from this area, the Chuckchi and Lamut districts which form the Chukot peninsula, jutting out into the Bering Sea.[2] The inhabitants are also mostly reindeer herders and again have a tradition that large manlike creatures exist there. The Lamuts call them Mirygdy ('broad-shoulders'), and describe

the creature as very tall with no neck, hairy, and secretive. If a
hunter should leave part of his kill to be retrieved the next day he
will return to find it gone and big footprints surrounding the
location. Apparently the creature eats raw meat, but, like a primate,
uses its hands to tear off pieces and put them in its mouth, not
tearing and chewing at it like a wolf. The Mirygdy is seen only in
summer (hardly surprising since this is sub-arctic tundra) and is
never hunted. Another variety is Kiltanya ('goggle-eye'), which has
big eyes, a narrow bridge to its nose and long footprints (*c.* 18 in.),
showing a narrow heel but ordinary toes. It, too, lives in the
mountains, eats meat and poaches the kills of hunters, and has
never been known to trouble man. A local policeman, also a Lamut,
told the story that not long before the last war an old man and
woman, living at the top of the Maina river, were approached two
nights in a row in November or December by something which
made the dogs bark a lot. It was very dark and they were unable to
see anything, but the next morning they found that the creature had
stolen some of their fish and left behind many human-looking
footprints about 1 'ell' (18 in.) long. The creatures are widely
reported from all over Chukotka territory but with different names,
not only Mirygdy and Kiltanya, but Teryk ('dawn man'),
Girkychavyl'in ('swift-runner'), Arynk, Arysa ('plainsman'),
Rekhem, Dzhulin ('sharphead'), and others less common. Many of
these 'Yeti' stories have a quasi-mythological ring, but they could
be founded on actual sightings.

The case for the existence of a tall, human-type wildman in
eastern Siberia, on the other hand, especially in the Yakut region
and the Verkhoyansk range, is considerably more convincing. Here
again we have a mixture of sightings made by the local peoples
(Tungus and Yakuts), together with the occasional observation
from outside, but the density of sightings is much greater than in
western Siberia and the wildmen are described in considerably
more detail. This really is an extreme climate – Verkhoyansk itself
has the distinction of being the coldest inhabited place on earth,
with a mean January temperature of $-59°F$ ($-50.5°C$) and a
recorded all-time low (1892) of $-90°F$ ($-67.7°C$). The winters are
very long as well as being very cold, and recorded sightings of the
wildmen (called Chuchunaa in this area[3]) come from all except the

two coldest months when presumably everybody, human and hominid alike, remains in hibernation as much as possible. The Verkhoyansk mountains stretch for hundreds of miles and are mostly unexplored. Much of the area remains unmapped, and even the heights of most of the mountains are still not known. Almost anything which could survive such extreme climatic conditions could have remained undetected here for thousands of years, and it is only with the post-war exploitation of Siberian mineral and forestry resources that anyone, apart from the few reindeer herders, has travelled here at all.

The sightings of Chuchunaa occur within a sharply defined area between the upland massifs east of the rivers Yana and Indigirka, with a concentration in the Verkhoyansk and Poloustnaya ranges. The following account is a typical example of a sighting made by one of the Tungus reindeer herders, in this case Tat'yana Il'inichna Zakharova:

After the Revolution, in the 1920s, the inhabitants of our village met a Chuchunaa, while gathering berries. He too was plucking berries with both hands and stuffing them in his mouth, and when he saw the people he stood up straight. He was very tall and lean, say over 2 m. He was dressed in a deer skin, and was barefoot. He had very long arms and dishevelled hair on his head. He had a big face, like a man's but dark. His forehead was small and hung over his eyes like a peaked cap. He had a big chin, broad and much bigger than a man's. All in all he was like a man, but of much greature stature. After a second he ran off. He ran very quickly, leaping high after every third step.

The report is interesting for various reasons and, like most of the Yakut sightings as well, is precisely located geographically and chronologically. It seems obvious that this Chuchunaa was a hominid, moreover one of the few referred to as wearing clothes (perhaps a cultural adaptation to the severe climate?). The eating of vegetable foods has been noted before for the Almas, as has the overhanging forehead and big jaw. But the height recorded in this and other published accounts of the Chuchunaa is considerably greater than that of the Almas.

Like all wildmen, the Chuchunaa has attracted a motley collection of folktales, and sometimes these can be distinguished as embroidery around a genuine sighting. There are many variations on the basic Chuchunaa stories – for example, one account given by the Tungus of Us-Yana is about a Chuchunaa who broke into a barn where food supplies were being stored and stole the lot. Unfortunately for him it had snowed that same night and in the morning the Tungus followed the tracks to a cave in the mountains, where they found the Chuchunaa eating his ill-gotten gains. Unarmed and unable to resist, 'he just fell as though begging for mercy, said something in an inarticulate language like the cry of an animal and bared his teeth'. It availed him nothing, the Tungus ran him through with a spear. Many people report hearing the cries and penetrating whistles when travelling in the mountains and there are other accounts of hunters who killed them.

Chuchunaa appear not only in folktales, but also in the infinitely more prosaic minutes of Party secretaries and reports to committees. Indeed, a 1928 record shows both the Commission on Yakut Affairs of the All-Russian Central Executive Committee and the Central Committee of the Communist Party taking an interest in them, and one Commission member (A.N. Asatkin from Vladimirskii) is on record as having expressed surprise in Moscow that no one had taken an interest in these people before.

Some local people are apparently of the opinion that the Chuchunaa population includes both powerful strong individuals and a few that seem thin and rather weak, and they suggest that the weak ones are ill, suffering from a particular disease. Similar accounts have been collected by the occasional scientific visitor. One such says that an alternative name in the south of eastern Siberia for the Chuchunaa is Mulen, and that they closely resemble primitive people.[5] Apparently Mulen have been known to follow travellers in the Dyuzhugdzhur range and wait for them to stop for the night and pitch their tents. After the fire has been lit and supper eaten the Mulen will creep up, sometimes armed with a bow or with stones, and attack. These Mulen are much feared by the local people and at times killed by them. The description is interesting.[6]

He is less than the average man in height [others say more]. His hair is unkempt, and the greater part of his face is covered in hair. He wears animal skins with the pelt outside. He wears something similar to deerskin boots and a band is tied round his head as a headdress. Sometimes the clothing is of undressed hide, as with the coat, breeches and boots taken from a Mulen by the Tungus who had killed him, perhaps five or six years ago [*c.* 1930]. For armament he has a bow with about 100 feathered arrows with special heads of unknown construction. He carries them over his shoulder in a special sheath or bag [in a quiver]. A knife hangs from his belt, a metal one, like those produced by wild uncivilized peoples. He has fire-steel. Sometimes he has a spear with a head of unknown construction. [The Chuchunaa living in the north has knife, fire-steel and spear.] Often he is met with armed only with sticks and stones. He produces separate inarticulate noises. Stealing up to a travellers' camp or to the tents of the local inhabitants the Mulen shoots with his bow or throws stones. He is in the habit of shooting non-stop until he has exhausted all his arrows. When he has run out of arrows he flees. He shoots from 15–20 sazhen [35–47 yards]. They are supposed to live in caves.

Significantly, Mulen is also said to be a Tungus word for 'bandit'. Both the Yakuts and Tungus are quite reluctant to talk about such encounters if they have a fatal ending, since they fear a prosecution for murder. Local rumour also suggests that many Mulen were killed in Yakutia during the Russian Civil War, when people began to move into previously uninhabited areas. Chuchunaa-hunts were organized during Tsarist times and during the Second World War, resulting in the deaths of many, and secret burial of the corpses.

As early as March 1929 a report on Mulen and Chuchunaa was presented by two distinguished scientists to the Commission for the Discovery and Study of Natural and Antiquarian Curiosities attached to the Western Siberian section of the Russian Geographical Society. This recommended detailed work and suggested that systematic studies of these 'people' should be started before they all became extinct; but despite the occasional newspaper article and note in passing, very little was done until the work of Pushkarev in the 1970s, already mentioned in the context of the Yeti-like creature, which has revived interest. Even in the intervening period, however, people were collecting tales about them. Here is a story told by Ivan Ivanovitch Lukshin, noted by G.U. Ergis on 15 August 1955, in the village of Pokrovsk.[7] The man had had a secondary education, and was a former Soviet worker, now retired, living in Mal'zhegar settlement in the Olekmin region.

A Chuchunaa came to a Tungus family in winter, carrying another Chuchunaa on his back. He laid the man being carried on a stove-couch [Russians often sleep on the stove], and by gesture indicated 'This man has broken his leg'. He said, as it were, 'He crept up to a mountain goat standing at the top of a cliff and grabbed it by the horns. The mountain goat took fright and leapt from the cliff top on to the cliff face, and the man broke his leg in the fall.'

They stayed the winter with the family. The Chuchunaa with the broken leg lay all winter, and the leg healed but was left crooked. The fit Chuchunaa could run very swiftly, and was an excellent hunter. He would haul on to his shoulders wild deer and mountain goats he had killed. He hit them all with a shot from his bow; they say he didn't know firearms. He said [i.e., seemed to say with gestures] 'We live in the rocky mountains. We do not know fire. We live in caves. We live by hunting alone. We earn our living from wild deer, eat their meat raw, wear their hides. We wear the deerskin whole; the head as a hat, the forelegs for arms and the hind legs as breeches and shoes' – so he related, they say. Spring came, and one warm day the Chuchunaa went. The fit one left the house and ran west, and the lame Chuchunaa hopped after him on one leg. They did not take any food supplies for the journey. They said they would feed themselves by hunting en route.

What is one to make of these accounts? Clearly both Chuchunaa and Mulen are human, or hominid, and technologically considerably more advanced than other wildmen we have come across. A great deal is known about their appearance and habits. Although accounts differ somewhat in different parts of eastern Siberia, the archetypal Chuchunaa are described as tall, heavily built, dressed in skins and with long hair. They avoid the local inhabitants, and gain their food by hunting with the bow and arrow, although they sometimes raid people's cellars. They seem to lead a nomadic way of life – an annual migration south during the summer is attested – and are seen either singly or in small groups, in sparsely populated areas. They have the use of fire, and the penetrating whistle so often recurring in tales about them (although it is even more characteristic of the Yeti-like primate) has been thought to be a 'war cry'. They would also seem to be on the road to extinction. As early as 1933 Professor P. Dravert made a plea for the hunting of these wild people to be abolished, claiming that like all citizens of the USSR they must have the protection of the law. But little has been done.

Are the Chuchunaa/Mulen undiscovered and unclassified 'primitive' people? The region where they live is probably the least-explored place in the world, and the survival of tribes who live by hunting in similarly remote areas, for example in the Amazon basin or New Guinea, is a matter of historical record. It has been suggested that the Chuchunaa in fact represent members of the nationalities already present in Siberia who have become 'barbarized' – who have become wildmen for some reason. Quite why any such regression should have taken place, especially in so harsh an environment where the benefits of our technological society may mean the difference between survival and extinction, cannot be satisfactorily explained. In any case, it would be unprecedented for an entire people of fully human stock to lose the power of speech and revert to communication using the 'inarticulate cries' commonly described for the Chuchunaa and Mulen.

More plausible is the idea that these Siberian hominids represent some earlier stage in human evolution, perhaps Neanderthal man. Their use of weapons of metal (albeit primitive) might indeed suggest Neanderthals who have experienced some degree of technological evolution, and thus answer one frequently-raised objection to the identification of any wildmen as Neanderthals, namely that there are few reports of tool-using behaviour, which suggests cultural regression. But the Chuchunaa, usually reported to be over 6 ft 6 in. tall, are really too big for the average Neanderthaler (typical height 5 ft 6 in.). Besides – as will be shown in the next chapter – there are stronger grounds for linking Neanderthals with Almas, and on present evidence Almas do not appear to be the same as Chuchunaa. Mulen and Chuchunaa therefore remain for the moment an unresolved mystery, linked in some way to the human family tree, but precisely how we do not know. Skeletal remains have apparently sometimes been found, particularly in the Adycha basin which is the Chuchunaa heartland, and if any of these could be examined scientifically the riddle might be solved.

*Chapter 9*
# Almas and
# Neanderthals

The suggestion that wildmen might be some kind, or kinds, of surviving primitive hominid is not a new one. The 18th-century zoologist, Linnaeus, believed, as we have seen, that mankind consisted of two species, civilized man (*Homo sapiens*) and wild man (*Homo troglodytes*), and in the 20th century Boris Porshnev developed the thesis in a number of articles and books. The problem with Porshnev's theories is that he tended to view all living wildmen as part of the Troglodyte family, despite the fact that some sightings quite clearly refer to non-human, apelike species. The foregoing chapters on the Yeti and Sasquatch should by now have made it evident that these creatures, whatever they may be, are not hominids – are not, that is, *manlike* creatures, any more than gorillas or chimpanzees are. But what about the reports of Almas in Mongolia, the Caucasus and the Pamirs – could they be relict hominids? Porshnev's firm belief was that Neanderthal man survived in Asia, and it is the purpose of this chapter to examine that claim, and the possible link with the Almas.

What is meant by the term 'Neanderthal'? It may be used as an evolutionary grade, an anthropological state or a biological description, but here I shall apply it to all those hominids whose remains can be shown to bear a close resemblance to the famous type-fossil of *Homo sapiens neanderthalensis* found in 1856 in a cave in the Neander valley near Düsseldorf. Unfortunately this first skeleton ever to be discovered was of an extreme type (the so-called 'classic' Neanderthal type), which has conditioned both public and expert views of Neanderthal appearance ever since. The 'classic' Neanderthals evolved after 70,000 years ago in Europe as a specialized response to cold and harsh conditions there at that time. But the original form of the species appeared much earlier – perhaps around 125,000 years ago, or even twice that if skull fragments from

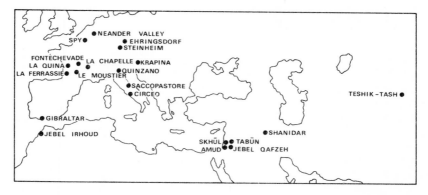

NEANDER VALLEY
SPY
EHRINGSDORF
STEINHEIM
FONTÉCHEVADE
LA QUINA
LA CHAPELLE
KRAPINA
LA FERRASSIE
LE MOUSTIER
QUINZANO
SACCOPASTORE
CIRCEO
TESHIK-TASH
GIBRALTAR
JEBEL IRHOUD
SHANIDAR
SKHŪL
AMUD
TABŪN
JEBEL QAFZEH

24 *Major Neanderthal sites in Europe and Western Asia.*

Swanscombe in Kent can be classified as being from an early Neanderthal. The 'non-classic' Neanderthals spread over much of Europe, the Near East and Asia, and formed the bulk of the Neanderthal population which dominated Eurasia until 30,000 years ago. In the 19th century, however, it was assumed that the western European 'classic' Neanderthals were the typical representatives of the species.

The head shape of the 'classic' Neanderthals was very distinctive, a long low-vaulted skull with strongly marked eyebrow ridges, receding chin, prominent jaw and large teeth, very different from the vertical forehead and rounder skull of modern man. These features were thought by some early anatomists to be Mongoloid, and they suggested that the Neander valley creature was not a fossil man at all, but the comparatively recent possessor of a flattened skull and bow legs; possibly a Mongolian Cossack whose presence in the cave could be explained by the hypothesis that he had deserted from the Russian army after it had driven Napoleon across the Rhine in 1814, and crawled into the cave to die. Hardly anyone, even geologists of the calibre of the 'father of modern geology', Charles Lyell, would admit that the fossil might be genuinely old, much less represent an ancestor of modern man. It was unfortunate that this first Neanderthal should have been found without any associated stone tools or the bones of extinct animals which would have hinted at its antiquity. It was not until another similar skeleton was unearthed at Spy in Belgium some ten years later that a compromise had to be reached, but even though the Spy fossil *did*

25 The dating of the major Neanderthal finds.

have the necessary tools and fauna the resemblance between the two skeletons was first dismissed as being accidental. Later finds made in the fossil-rich limestone cave sites of the Dordogne in central France between 1908 and 1921 changed the picture a good deal, but scientists are still not sure whether Neanderthal man is our direct ancestor, from whom we evolved, or simply a close relative.

What did Neanderthal man actually look like? There can be no single reconstruction applicable to all varieties of the hominid, since a population of Neanderthals would have included as great a range of shapes, sizes and colours as any modern group of people. The average Neanderthal was shorter than we (about 5 ft 6 in.), with a barrel chest and heavily muscled frame, but many variations of this type exist. The best we can do is to take individual skeletons and build up individual portraits from them.

A great deal of work has now been done on the complicated relationship between a person's bone structure and his actual appearance. Apart from the basic features of the skull we also need details of the bodily proportions, stance and posture. Different generations of anatomists have had different preconceived ideas about what their own reconstruction *should* look like. The relatively complete skeleton of an adult male found in 1908 at La Chapelle-aux-Saints in France has been used as a model for Neanderthal appearance many times. Unfortunately the first reconstruction was carried out by a French palaeontologist, Marcellin Boule, who tried to make the result as close in appearance to an ape as he could. The spinal column was reassembled in such a way that it would have been impossible for the creature ever to have walked fully upright, and the head was positioned so far forward on the neck that the man would have appeared to be a hunchback, shambling along on bent knees and walking on the outside edge of his feet. It is not surprising that for many years after this the Neanderthals were viewed as aberrant evolutionary sidelines, long since extinct. Boule did, however, recognize some of the characteristic Neanderthal features already described, and he calculated the brain capacity of the fossil correctly to be 1450 cc. (The generally accepted values for Neanderthal brains vary from 1300 to 1600 cc, comparable with modern man.) A re-appraisal of the skeleton from La Chapelle by two American anthropologists in 1957 confirmed that it was indeed the remains of a man aged between perhaps forty and fifty, but he had suffered from chronic arthritis of the jaw, legs and spine, and allowing for this there was no evidence that his posture had been different from that of modern man.

New discoveries about Neanderthal anatomy and new specimens have been only partly responsible for a change in the appearance of the models; excavations have also shown that Neanderthals had a highly developed social sense, making an apelike appearance inappropriate. Ritual burials found at sites such as Teshik-Tash in Russia and La Ferrassie in France demonstrate a fully human concern for the dead and belief in an afterlife. But it is quite possible that today we have gone to the opposite extreme. The Neanderthal model produced by the anthropologist Richard Leakey in 1978 is fully human in appearance. The extensive body hair and mane felt necessary by earlier restorers has vanished, and the artist has tried to emphasize the tough, rugged, mountaineering-type body form.[1]

An exhibition, 'Man's Place in Human Evolution', on display in the British Museum (Natural History) in London, includes an excellent reconstruction of a Neanderthal woman, based on the 41,000-year-old female skeleton from Tabun, near Mount Carmel in Israel. This model took nearly three months to reconstruct, starting with careful measurements to determine accurate height and length of limbs. After the correct anatomical details had been determined, the next step was to make a sculptor's armature, the supporting framework round which the model would eventually be built. In this case it was made from wood and steel, the outline of the shape being added from scrim (layers of sacking) soaked in plaster and polystyrene. Plasticine was used for the final touches – skin texture, hair and all the fine contours of the face. But this plasticine model was only the first stage in the process – a mould had to be made from which the final product would be cast in glass-reinforced plastic and painted ready for display. The finished model seems slimmer and less robust than Leakey's Neanderthal, but anatomically it is also quite correct and bears a marked resemblance to descriptions of Almas.

The trickiest part of the whole process is getting a suitable expression for the face, since it is difficult to reproduce in a static model the constantly changing play of expression on the human face, or even to decide on facial contours and the size and shape of ears, nose and eyes. Until recently anatomists thought that these characteristics of a person's face could never be reconstructed from the skeleton alone, but a Russian anatomist, Mikhail Gerasimov, showed that they were wrong, producing some of the most famous (and best) reconstructions of Neanderthal appearance ever. The technique he invented was evolved using more recent human individuals, where sufficient documentation existed so that he could use X-rays, photographs and portraits to check the accuracy of his results. Gerasimov placed great emphasis on the replication of each individual group of muscles, carefully calculating their size and position, using anatomical evidence provided by modern examples. He achieved remarkable results when asked to work 'blind', reconstructing the facial appearance of bodies in unsolved murder cases, and he also produced a series of reconstructions of historical Russian nobles, including Tsar Ivan the Terrible, which closely match extant portraits. It seems likely that his Neanderthal models also approximate very closely to their owners' original appearance.

It has been suggested that Neanderthal man's broad face was accompanied by a big nose which warmed cold air in its extra-large nasal sinuses. The reason he had such a broad face could have been because of the type of food he ate. The relationship between diet and appearance is quite a close one, and changes in diet can indeed cause small changes in the appearance of a group of people after several generations. The tough meat and vegetable foods which Neanderthals consumed would certainly have required large, strong teeth, and the heavy brow ridges could have been there to support the massive jaw muscles. Similarly, the bun-shaped swelling at the back of the head probably acted as a counterweight to the big face. These facial features – the heavy brow ridges, the large jaw – closely resemble descriptions of Almas.

The short, stocky Neanderthal body is also often viewed as a climatic adaptation, and indeed modern Eskimos have similar physiques. But some stocky Neanderthals lived in tropical and semi-tropical conditions, and in the very cold phase at the end of the Ice Age, Europe was inhabited by populations of modern-looking men whose bodily proportions were similar to our own, so the cold-adaptation theory is not so simple after all.

Bones can also give us unexpected insights into the Neanderthal way of life. We find, for example, that their ankle bones frequently show a modification called the 'squatting facet' common in hunting communities today, indicating that Neanderthals spent a good deal of time crouched round a camp fire. We also know that they led an active and sometimes dangerous life, hunting animals including mountain goat or ibex which inhabited rocky mountainous regions and required skill and cunning in order to be caught. It is not, perhaps, surprising that Neanderthal remains often show evidence of numerous fractures, but the fact that many of these are well healed suggests a knowledge of at least simple anatomy.

The most common diseases (those that have left some evidence) seem to have been rickets and arthritis, the latter being very common even in the bones of Neanderthals who lived in quite warm climates. Rickets, a vitamin-deficiency disease which produces characteristically bowed legs, was common during the Industrial Revolution when children in smoky towns suffered from a lack of sunlight. It can also be caused by a lack of milk, which is a good source of vitamin D, but it seems difficult to explain why it was so common in Neanderthal times. Neanderthal children would almost certainly have continued to be breast-fed until the age of at least two or three, but after that it is unlikely that they would ever have had any more milk, although smaller amounts of vitamin D can be obtained from meat. Lack of sunlight in gloomy interglacial twilight might, of course, have been a contributory factor. Neanderthals had not invented the bow, fish-hook or harpoon, so were rarely able to catch wildfowl, fish or seafood, which are important sources of vitamin D. With the arrival of modern man, by contrast, these foods became common additions to the diet, and the incidence of rickets decreased dramatically.

The rugged Neanderthal lifestyle seems to have contributed to a high death rate among infants. Twenty out of the forty-five Neanderthal burials from Western Europe and the Near East examined in a recent study proved to be of children or infants, the most common age at death being five or six. This is rather peculiar since it is after the supposedly hazardous years of early childhood, when modern infant mortality figures are at their highest. Perhaps burials of younger children – whose bones are extremely fragile –

26 *Neanderthal and modern man compared. Note the short, strongly-muscled Neanderthal physique and heavy-browed face.*

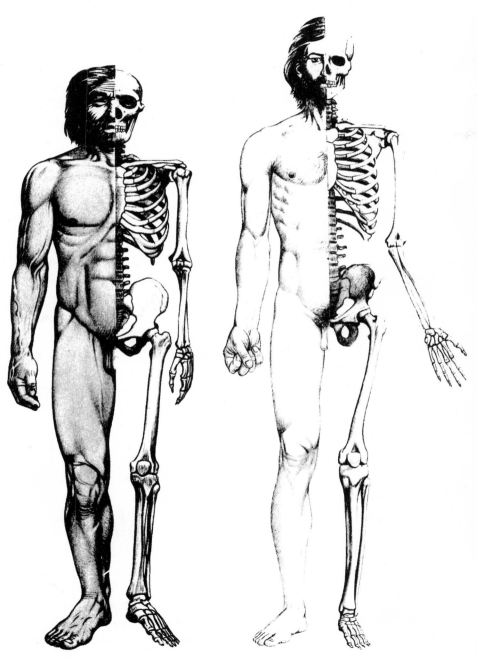

were missed in older excavations. The Iraqi site of Shanidar yielded a skeleton of a Neanderthal baby which was only $1\frac{3}{4}$ in. thick. The common age at death could, however, correspond to the time when Neanderthal children were making their first forays out from the home base, exposing them to dangers that had previously been avoided. In modern hunting societies, such as the Bushmen of the Kalahari Desert, children need to be physically precocious to keep up; by the time our children are attending nursery school Bushmen infants are out hunting with their fathers, with attendant risk of accidents.

Even if you survived the dangerous years of childhood as a Neanderthal, you were not likely to have a long life. Out of the 150 or so Neanderthals known, only 5 per cent survived to more than fifty. Neanderthal men tended to die between the ages of thirty and forty and Neanderthal women younger still, probably in childbirth. But then even anatomically modern people did not generally live beyond the age of forty until the 19th century.

In the cave of Kiik-Koba, one of a series of important Russian Neanderthal sites in the Crimea – significantly close to modern sightings of Almas – a burial of a one-year-old child was found associated with the remains of an adult Neanderthal, possibly a female. The adult skelton was especially interesting since the bones of the right leg, both feet and one hand were quite well preserved, a rare occurrence. Neanderthal hands were in some ways rather primitive. They had powerful grips, as one might expect, but they were not as flexible as ours. For example, it would have been difficult for Neanderthals to hold pencils or turn keys, since their thumbs could not reach all the other fingers to give a sufficiently precise grip. The foot bones are more similar to ours, although the Neanderthal foot was broader, with rather a short big toe. Actual examples of Neanderthal footprints even survive in the mud floor of a sealed cave at Toirano near Rome, found during the course of quarrying in 1950.[3]

Neanderthal tools include a wide variety of scrapers and borers, some of which seem to have been used for skins and some for working wood, bone and antler, and at least two sites have produced bone awls for making clothes. Neanderthals living in Europe and Asia during very cold periods would have required

clothing from head to toe. Modern hunters often take great pride in their garments, no matter how simple, and it seems likely that Neanderthals were equally fussy, certainly about their furs. Various carnivores, including bear and lion, seem to have been hunted entirely for their pelts. The Hungarian site of Erd, which was occupied seasonally about 40,000 years ago, has yielded the remains of over 500 cave bears. Apparently the hunters visited the area at the right time of year to catch the bears after their annual hibernation, but what they did with the large number of bearskins obtained is something of a mystery. They must surely have had too many for their own clothing needs, and the surplus could have been exchanged with other groups for some sought-after commodity. If this is so it would be the earliest evidence for trade – or more accurately barter – an activity that Almas also apparently indulge in.

One of the most controversial questions about Neanderthal man is, could he speak? As early as 1889 it was suggested that Neanderthal speech was more primitive than ours. Modern man could never have developed his high degree of social organization and civilization without being able to communicate detailed, abstract ideas. Simple warnings are uttered by other primates, but man is the only creature to use sound to communicate ideas. Although some primates use a simple visual 'language', with up to forty-five distinguishable types of gesture, and chimpanzees even convey compound thoughts by adding together strings of gestures, the language of human speech is infinitely more complex.[4]

It is not yet clear what the precise relationship is between brain size, brain internal organization and the ability to make symbols for facts, but it must be significant that the only animals which can do this have human-sized brains (like dolphins). The gradual increase in brain capacity which took place during human evolution must be related to increased linguistic ability, but this does not mean that speech and language developed at the same time.

Most scientists think that Neanderthal man could speak. Two American academics, however, believe he had only about 10 per cent of the phonetic ability of modern man and produced only a very restricted range of sounds. Philip Lieberman, Professor of Linguistics at the University of Connecticut, and Edmund Crelin, of the Yale University Medical School, reached this astonishing conclusion in a controversial piece of research. Crelin studied the different hominid vocal tracts and concluded that the Neanderthal tract (based on the specimen from La Chapelle-aux-Saints) was much closer to that of an adult ape or human infant than a modern human adult. It is possible to programme a computer to explore the relationship between the size and shape of the vocal tract and the type of sounds which it will produce starting with modern vocal tracts and modern languages. Lieberman did just this, and discovered that the consonants K and G would have been impossible for Neanderthal man, together with the vowels in words like BAR, BOO, BEEP and BOUGHT. Only the pitiful vowels in BIT, BAT, BET or BUT would have remained to form the basis of a language. This was not an experiment tried in isolation. Similar reconstructions were made of earlier fossils, including *Australopithecus* and the female from Steinheim in Germany who is particularly important since she represents the group of hominids we have previously referred to as *Homo erectus* – the basic population from which both Neanderthals and modern men evolved. The vocal tract of *Australopithecus* was found to be identical to that of a modern ape, much as one might have expected, but that of the Steinheim woman proved to be similar in size and shape to that of modern man, unlike the Neanderthal reconstruction which was much more primitive. If Lieberman and Crelin are right, then Neanderthals were at a serious evolutionary disadvantage. Their work has been much criticized, however. For instance, the only modern language Lieberman used as the basis of his experiments was American-English, even though different languages require different ranges of vowels and consonants.

Much current research is focussing on the relationship between speech ability and intelligence. In addition to the correct shape of vocal tract, a certain brain power is required, and it seems that about 1,000 cc of brain tissue distributed in the right way is essential – well within the capacity of Neanderthals, who had relatively large brains for their body size. There is much speculation about the relative roles of the right and left hemispheres of the brain in speech, and a Russian authority on this matter, Veronika Kochetkova, has just produced a book tracing the evolution of man's brain. It is interesting to note that the parts of the brain connected with speech, image-making, judgment and manual dexterity grew larger and more complicated *after* the Neanderthals. The transition to modern man would make complete sense if it could be shown that the evolution of fully articulate speech can be correlated with anatomical changes which took place at this time.

Not all Neanderthals can have had speech problems; the braincases from Broken Hill in Zimbabwe and Saccopastore in Italy show features which seem to resemble the skulls of modern man. The most extreme Neanderthal skull shape (as seen in the La Chapelle example) was not the norm for all Neanderthals. Lieberman and Crelin themselves reconstructed the vocal tract of a 'progressive' Neanderthal from one of the Mount Carmel sites in Israel, Skuhl V, and found that his vocal tract was modern. But even if *some* Neanderthals did not have fully articulate speech that is most interesting, since the 'classic' (extreme) forms are in many cases associated with precisely those rituals and ceremonies which one might think would demand speech. So how did they manage? One suggestion is that gestures would have been sufficient for communicating such complex ideas, just as it is today in deaf-and-dumb language. If some Neanderthals did have speech problems, it seems most likely that they made a greater use of gesture than we do. This evidence is immensely important for any attempt to link Neanderthals with living Almas. As we have observed in earlier chapters Almas, like Neanderthals, are apparently also incapable of speech, and have been known to supplement their inarticulate grunts with gestures.

What happened to the Neanderthals? We know that they were loosely organized into large super-tribal groups, and that between them the different forms dominated Europe, Asia and Africa from about 125,000 to 35,000 years ago. The scanty archaeological record indicates that this dominance came to an end in different areas at different times, and whatever the reason modern man (*Homo sapiens sapiens*) was in each case the successor. One theory sees two divergent non-modern (Neanderthaloid) evolutionary lines combining to produce a stock from which modern man emerged. This assumes that the 'classic' Neanderthals were not so different in physical appearance or skills from earlier, more primitive men that they could not breed with them, an assumption supported by recent work which shows that morphologically early Neanderthals more closely resemble modern man than the later ones.[5] A second school of thought sees the 'classic' strain being extinguished by evolving into modern man, although quite how this might have been accomplished is not clear. Three alternatives remain:

1  that the 'classic' Neanderthals became extinct when modern man arrived;
2  that they effectively disappeared because of social and cultural merging and inbreeding; or
3  that they were forced out of the best hunting grounds (and thus the archaeological record) into remote areas where small populations could have survived.

Any combination of these three theories can also be considered.[6]

The idea that Neanderthal man *must* be extinct because modern man can be the only surviving hominid is outmoded biological arrogance. One has only to consider the large number of primates (for example, *Rhinopithecus*, the snub-nosed langur, and *Pan paniscus*, the African pygmy chimpanzee) which have been discovered in the last 150 years to realize this. It can be said, with some truth, that yesterday's myths are today's scientific discoveries, and this has certainly been the case with the mountain gorilla (*Gorilla gorilla beringei*), whose existence was dismissed in the 19th century as improbable. Ultimately it is a matter of the feasibility of survival.

The question of whether or not it was possible for Neanderthal man to evolve into modern man over a relatively short period of time hinges upon whether there is any evolutionary mechanism by which this might have been accomplished; but there is little support for the theory. It has been suggested that the 'modernization' of the Neanderthal head could be a result of alterations in the vocal tract as the upper part of the throat changed into a pharynx capable of producing the full human sound range. It is not, however, clear why such changes did not occur during the preceding thousands of years, or why, once initiated, they progressed so quickly.

Recent work suggests that the relationship between Neanderthal man and *Homo sapiens sapiens* during the crucial period

55,000–29,000 years ago was very complicated indeed, and considerable cultural and technological overlap is suggested rather than straightforward replacement. Unless one accepts that very rapid physical evolution took place at this time coexistence seems most likely, with Neanderthal and early *sapiens* bands occupying different territories. The degree of contact, however, whether by trade or inter-band mating, remains pure speculation. There is ample evidence that Neanderthal bands occupied well-defined hunting territories and that bands with different tool-making traditions could exist separately within a given region at the same time. All this adds up to the fact that the total extinction of Neanderthal man by 'extermination' is unlikely, since historical parallels (for example, the North American Indians of the Great Plains) suggest that the weaker group generally retreats slowly into less desirable and more remote areas which remain uncompeted for. It is in precisely those areas that the archaeological record is most sparse and where, as one might expect, most of the records of Almas originate (the Mongolian Altai, Tien Shan range, the Pamirs, the Caucasus). The relatively sophisticated social organization of Neanderthals would seem to conflict with what we know of Almas, but the evidence is very slight. There can be no question of present-day Almas living the sort of life that classic Neanderthals enjoyed in their heyday, although tantalizing glimpses (like the Almas seen butchering an ibex) do suggest continuity. If Almas are Neanderthals, driven into remote areas where they have survived for what is really quite an insignificant period of time, some degree of cultural recession is inevitable; to what degree this has occurred it is impossible to say.

During a visit to Outer Mongolia in 1979 I had the opportunity of tentatively testing the possible link between the Almas of the region and Mousterian (Neanderthal) sites there.[7] My travels, some 1,900 miles in all, zigzagged across the junction area between the high Altai mountains and the flat, arid Gobi plains from which they rise so abruptly. In the really high mountains the permanent snow cover stood at about 12,000 ft during my visit in August/September, and the dry, raw cold was aggravated by a biting wind. The mountain air is amazingly clear and one treads paths made by the moufflon with the feeling that no one has ever been there before. Of course they have, but the Mongol nomads who herd yaks and goats across the mountains on horseback see no reason to stay in these inhospitable areas – in some cases they are actually afraid to do so, since Buddhist tradition says that the mountains are the abode of demons. They are certainly a haven for rare animals, such as the wild camel and wild horse of the Gobi and the supposed Gobi bear, although zoologists are coming to the conclusion that the second is now extinct and the third may never have existed at all. The same cannot be said for the snow leopard (*Panthera uncia*), a shy, exotic and beautiful creature, with mottled blue-white fur, which was known for centuries only from legend and old books, and now survives in small numbers in these remote mountains as well as in Tibet.

The population of Mongolia is very small (about one and a half million) and dispersed over a wide area three times the size of France. The mountains are rugged and honeycombed with caves. There is plenty of food (ibex, moufflon and small game), water, and good raw materials for tools. Half the Neanderthals of western Europe could have ended up here and nobody would have discovered them. Indeed, it would be more surprising if no traces of hominid activity had been found, since the rocks of the area include jasper, chalcedony and agate, much favoured by Neanderthals whenever they could find them. At some sites tools made from these materials were used until they were literally worn out, and even then the small chips were resharpened again. The Mousterian tool kits that I found in open-air sites in the Altai river terraces were made from these rocks, and include scrapers, rough chopping tools and some small, neatly re-touched flakes.[8] As yet we have no method of obtaining firm absolute dates from them since there is no associated bone or wood which could be tested by the radiocarbon method, but we are able to compare the styles with assemblages from other areas whose dates *are* known. As one might expect, the Mongolian material seems rather primitive compared with the more soigné tools from the classic French culture sequences.

The Mongolian sites appear to be quite late in date for the Mousterian, some less than 20,000 years old. They may, indeed, be even more recent, since many of the tools are fresh and surprisingly unworn if they have been resting on the surface for that length of time. They are always found in the foothills of the mountains, below the permanent snow cover, as though the people were living there to take advantage of different environments for good hunting and reasonable access to better-class rocks for tool-making. None of the caves in the high mountains have yet been investigated archaeologically, but it would be very interesting to do so. We know from other sites that Neanderthals were particularly fond of mountain-fringe areas, as in the Shanidar cave in northern Iraq for example, or the many sites in the Dordogne and European Russia. The Altai foothills are exactly the place where one might have predicted that Neanderthal man once lived, a hypothesis which was happily confirmed by fieldwork.

The local people, who have, as one might expect, an intimate knowledge of their own territories, were quite happy to talk about stone tools (and about Almas), although they thought my interest in both to be strange. The remoteness of the area cannot be overstressed; in some places I was the first non-Russian they had ever met, and of course the existence of Britain was quite unknown and the number of yaks kept on average by British families a matter for constant enquiry. This means that the stories and identifications I received from the local people are unlikely to have been biassed by contact with outside sources, as definitely happens, for example, when visitors try to question the Sherpas of Nepal about the Yeti.

My first line of approach was to show examples of Neanderthal tools to the people and ask whether they had ever seen anything like them in the area. Inevitably they had, and could show me the precise location. Secondly, I asked whether they themselves knew anything about the tools, and here I obtained the same answer from a number of widely-separated groups. All agreed that the tools had been used by people 'who used to live in this area before us' and who now 'live in the mountains'. The name given to these people never varied; the locals called them either the people of Tuud or, when asked to elaborate, gave them the name Almas or one of its local variations. I am now prepared to accept the reality of the Almas, and we can prove the existence of Neanderthal man in this area at some period. The connection between the two is hypothetical but distinctly possible.

The question of whether or not Almas may be relict (surviving)

Neanderthals is still open, as it has been since Porshnev first presented his opinions on the matter to the Commission for the Study of the Snowman of the Soviet Academy of Sciences (Moscow) in 1958. His suggestion cannot be confirmed or denied until we have a living, breathing Almas to study (or at least a well-preserved corpse). For me there is no question of whether they exist – I find the evidence compelling – but only of how they should be classified.

# Epilogue

Wildmen certainly exist in our minds, in our art and in our literature. They exist as the terrifying creatures with which we people the unknown world. They exist as the satyrs of antiquity, the wodewose of the Middle Ages or the socially rebellious young men of the 20th century. Each generation creates wildmen in its own image. In the modern era fear of the hairy outcast has largely given way to fear of mutant wildmen and freaks, from Frankenstein's monster to the superhuman mutants of John Wyndham's science fantasy, *The Midwich Cuckoos*. Perhaps this reflects the growing realization that we have it in our power to produce monsters either accidentally (by administering drugs such as thalidomide) or deliberately (radioactive fallout from nuclear bombs). Chinese scientists are even trying – horrifying thought! – to create a 'near-human' ape by impregnating a chimpanzee with human sperm.[1]

But acknowledging the existence of psychological, literary or manmade wildmen is very different from acknowledging the existence of authentic wildmen as defined in this book – of genuine apemen or man-apes of as yet unclassified species. The mythological and folkloristic evidence put forward in Chapter 1 has little to offer when it comes to identifying such creatures. Medieval man certainly *believed* in wildmen, just as he believed in witches; but today historians view the rise and fall of the European witch craze as a social phenomenon, not as evidence that real physical witches existed: it seems equally unlikely that medieval wildmen were anything more than social outcasts and recluses decked out in mythological garb. Of course, Porshnev's thesis was that a *known* hominid species – Neanderthal man – had actually survived, and could be observed in the myths and legends of ancient Greece and Rome. There is something in human nature which makes us reluctant to accept that anything (including ourselves) can come to a full stop, leaving no apparent trace. Legends which tell of the survival of great religious prophets – Jesus, for instance – or charismatic leaders such as Hitler, are deep-rooted in the human psyche. This does not, however, make the legends any the more true or believable. There is simply no convincing link or comparison that can be made between the half-human, half-animal satyr figure and the wholly human – if not wholly *modern* human – Neanderthal man, much as we would like to make the connection. As for the account of the 18th-century Rumanian wild boy cited by Bayanov and Burtsev as clear proof of Neanderthal survival, the deformities ascribed to the wretched child seem to me to be those of a mental defective rather than of a relict hominid.

Another kind of human 'deformity' – the biological abnormality which causes certain people to become giants – has sometimes been linked with the wildman phenomenon. Cases are known of human giants up to about 9 ft tall. There also seems to be a basic human need to invent giant-sized figures for the purpose of being afraid of them, from the Cyclops in Homer's *Odyssey* to *Gulliver's Travels*. But if there is a connection between wildmen and giants (actual or fictional), Neanderthal man and the Almas must be ruled out of court, since they are both too small. Only the Yeti would qualify, and the putative link between him and giants is remote indeed, particularly in view of the very definite apelike, not manlike, qualities attributed to the Yeti.

If both apelike and manlike wildmen do exist, it seems that the strongest evidence comes from recent or near-recent sightings and descriptions. To turn the discussion on its head for one moment, it is easy to see that the assumption that they do *not* exist rests on the belief that our world is so thoroughly explored, so well charted that no unclassified creatures will ever be discovered. It is equally easy to demonstrate how ill-founded this assumption is. There are still vast areas of the world whose natural history is almost completely unknown, and over the last 150 years dozens of large animals have come to light, including some, like the okapi, which were thought to be extinct. Most were known from native reports which were initially disbelieved. At least twenty new mammals are described and classified annually.[2] If non-human species can be discovered, is it so unlikely that closer relatives live somewhere on our planet?

Although the best evidence comes from Asia and North America, other parts of the world have their modern wildman legends too. The Orangpendek (also known as the Sedapa) of the lowland forests of Sumatra and Borneo is said to be a small hairy manlike creature which could – like the Almas – be a survivor from an earlier stage of human evolution. A Yeti-equivalent in the mountains of Borneo was also reported some twenty years ago, a relative perhaps of the so-called Orang-dalam of Malaysia, which is reputedly 6–10 ft tall, much the same height as the Yeti. Bernard Heuvelmans has recently published a book called *Les bêtes humaines d'Afrique* (1980), in which he discusses stories of undiscovered wildmen in Africa. But the Asian and North American evidence is still indubitably the strongest.

Sightings, footprints, droppings and hairs are the sum total of the evidence for the apelike Yeti, yet despite this they provide a surprisingly consistent picture over an area which has become hugely extended by recent reports from China and the Pamirs. For instance, the footprints ($13\frac{3}{4}$ in. long and $6\frac{3}{4}$ in. broad) seen by Lord Hunt in the Himalayas in 1978 now match to an extraordinary extent those found in the Pamirs in 1979 ($13\frac{1}{4} \times 6\frac{1}{4}$ in.). The Chinese footprints which we know about are larger ($15\frac{1}{4}$–$18\frac{3}{4}$ in.), but again can be closely compared with another example ($19\frac{1}{4}$ in.) from the Pamirs found in 1981, not to mention the – admittedly vague – reference to an 18-in. footprint from eastern Siberia. The evidence of sightings, droppings and hairs is more equivocal, but cumulatively nonetheless impressive as we have seen. So what, ultimately, are the assumed characteristics, distribution and behaviour patterns of the Yeti, and how do they compare with those of the Sasquatch? Broadly speaking the Yeti seems to be a large, hairy primate, often well over 6 ft 6 in. tall, which is omnivorous, nocturnal and has a high-pitched cry. Most reports refer to solitary Yetis, although groups have been seen, and the habitat seems to be the remote montane valleys and uplands of east and west Siberia, China, the Pamirs, the Himalayas and other parts of Asia. The long arms, tendency to walk or run occasionally on all fours, lack of speech and inability to use tools all mark out the Yeti as an apelike, not manlike, species.

These apelike qualities are common as well to the Sasquatch of the Pacific northwest coast of America, known also primarily from sightings, droppings and footprints, especially from Bossburg (one must discount the Patterson film until it can be demonstrated conclusively not to be a fake). It is significant that the recorded footprint range of the Sasquatch ($15-18\frac{1}{2}$ in.) closely matches that of the Yeti ($13-19\frac{1}{4}$ in.), and aspects of behaviour too, such as nocturnalism and the association of both the Siberian Yeti and Bigfoot with water, can be paralleled in the two continents. Even features such as coat colour, which might be taken to indicate clear differences, seem on the contrary to betoken broad similarities. The majority of Sasquatch have brown or black hair, although some have light coats; Chinese and Himalayan Yetis are reddish brown, while their Siberian counterparts tend to be black and the Pamirs variety silver-coated. This differentiation is no more than one would expect for a species spread over thousands of miles and many different latitudes. Moreover, if both Yetis and Sasquatch have evolved from the great ape *Gigantopithecus*, as we suspect, some separate development of features such as coat colour is to be expected as the different representatives of the species adapted to their new environments.

On the face of it, then, while some attributes of the Yeti and Sasquatch, such as enormous height or red glowing eyes, can be put down to the exaggeration inherent in folktales, the evidence of footprints recorded by reputable people suggests that there is a genuine enigma waiting to be solved by science.

The case for the existence of the manlike Almas is more convincing and yet less well substantiated. Here there are no droppings or hairs and few footprints which have been observed and analyzed by Western enthusiasts.

The regions where the creatures are reported – outer Mongolia, the Caucasus and the Pamirs – are too remote and inaccessible for Europeans to have visited them in the way they have the Himalayas. Instead, for the moment, we must rely on second-hand accounts of sightings. Ironically, if we had full access to all the evidence the Almas might appear much better substantiated than the Yeti. We now know that the Mongolian Professor Zhamtsarano spent decades at the beginning of this century plotting and recording evidence of the Almas in Outer Mongolia: his extensive material is today held in two inaccessible Russian archives in Leningrad and Ulan Ude. And the systematic research into the Caucasian Almas undertaken by Dr Kofman since 1960 likewise remains unpublished and unconfirmed in the West. Dr Kofman apparently took a cast of an Almas footprint in 1978 – the only one known – but neither a photograph nor any details have so far been published.

Against this unpromising background it is encouraging to note the consistency of many of the reports (few of which have the mythological overtones typical of countless Yeti stories). Almas are similar in height to modern man (perhaps slightly shorter than the average Westerner), although much hairier, with a characteristic head shape including a jutting-out jaw, receding chin and very prominent eyebrow ridges. The creatures are shy, avoiding contact with their modern neighbours, apparently able to use tools but incapable of coherent speech. They appear to be confined to high mountainous areas where there are a number of lakes, especially the Mongolian Altai ranges and the desert fringes of Dzungaria, with the distribution stretching westwards across the Tien Shan range of Sinkiang and ending in the foothills of the Caucasus. Reports go back to the 13th century and are remarkably similar in their content, but it would seem that the geographical distribution of Almas is shrinking under increasing pressure from our own species, and the area where they can still be found is confined to a small corner of the Mongolian Altai mountains. However, they are still being sighted, either as solitary individuals or as family groups, and would seem to be surviving by keeping out of our way as much as possible, which is not really very difficult, since the high mountains are not suitable for agriculture, or anything more than the occasional visit by nomadic herdsmen moving from pasture to pasture. Almas seem to eke out a living at a bare subsistence level by hunting small mammals and eating wild plants, unassisted by fire although with shelter available in the form of caves. A crucial point, however, is that they do not appear to be *afraid* of fire, unlike all non-human species.

This very simple lifestyle and the nature of their appearance suggests strongly that Almas might represent the survival of a prehistoric way of life, and perhaps even of an earlier form of man. The best candidate is undoubtedly Neanderthal man, who dominated Europe and Asia from 125,000 years ago and disappears mysteriously from the archaeological record 30,000 years ago. The characteristic skull shape – a long, low-vaulted cranium with prominent brow ridges and jutting jaw – is curiously reminiscent of descriptions of Almas, as is the recorded Neanderthal height of about 5 ft. 6 in. The theory that Neanderthal man had only a limited speech capacity also finds its parallel in reports of the Almas. Most telling of all, perhaps, is the intriguing overlap between Neander-thal sites and Almas-sightings around the Caucasus area, at Teshik-Tash in the Pamirs, and in Outer Mongolia as I discovered on my visit there in 1979. If one were hypothesizing that Neanderthals had retreated into remote regions in the face of the inexorable advance of modern man 30,000 years ago, these are just the sorts of areas where one might expect to find them.

There are nevertheless considerable difficulties with the equation Almas = Neanderthal man. Neanderthals were advanced members of the species *Homo sapiens*, who were the first to practise ritual burial of the dead, and may have had a developed social sense to the extent that they cared for the sick, wounded and elderly individuals. Moreover they used and made fire, as species of *Homo* had done for hundreds of thousands of years. None of these attributes and abilities seem to apply to Almas. They are culturally more primitive than Neanderthals ever were, and possible reasons for this should be carefully considered. There is nothing to stop human evolution taking a backward turn, and it may be that Almas are the result of just such a *volte face*. The concept of steady, unilinear evolution has recently been under attack by people who misunderstood Darwin to have said that evolution by means of natural selection was a slow but ineluctable process which acted on every creature, everywhere.[3] What he actually said was that natural selection (applicable to human and animal alike) acted slowly at long time intervals, but on only a few of the inhabitants of the same region. The idea of rather jerky evolution, bursts of activity separated by plateaux of inactivity which may have lasted for thousands or millions of years, is therefore not a new one. Its results are difficult to detect in either the geological or archaeological record, which tends to telescope events that happened hundreds or even thousands of years apart into a very small and tangled piece of stratigraphy. Certain species

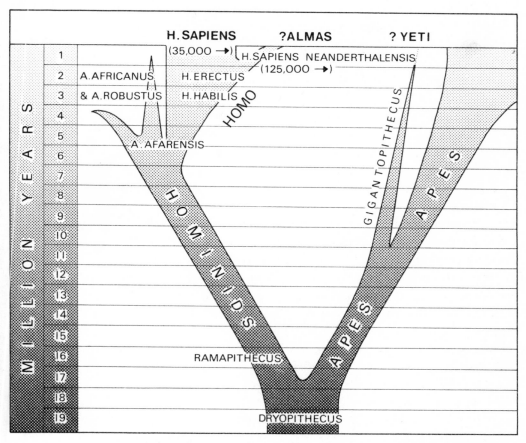

27 *A chart setting out the possible evolutionary relationship of the Almas, Yeti, modern man and the apes.*

seem to have remained stable for long periods, including early species of man. The history of human evolution is one of bursts of activity followed by lengthy pauses. To complicate matters there are generally several different kinds of hominids in existence at the same time.[4] Some species seem to have made sudden leaps forward (or backwards, or even sideways), and it is possible that modern Almas may represent such an event, an evolutionary backtracking or at least a substantial pause.

An alternative view, not so far discussed in these pages, is that the common ancestor of both Neanderthals and ourselves – *Homo erectus* – could somehow be equated with living Almas. The idea is not so fanciful as it might seem at first sight. *Homo erectus* evolved some $1\frac{1}{2}$ million years ago and, although he was an intelligent, upright-walking, tool-making hominid, he possessed certain of the superficially primitive characteristics of the Almas, such as short stature, hirsuteness and a heavily built face. We also have good archaeological evidence that he remained relatively stable in evolutionary terms for a very long period of time. Although superseded on the world stage by first the Neanderthals and then modern man, recent finds displaying unmistakable *Homo erectus* features made at Kow Swamp in Australia seem to suggest that he survived in that part of the world at any rate until a mere 10,000 years ago. Indeed it has been suggested that there are still a few representatives of *Homo erectus* in the largely unexplored interior of Australia,[5] accounting for the many descriptions of curious manlike or apelike creatures from that region. But the evidence linking Almas and *Homo erectus* is tenuous to say the least, and requires a much more widespread survival of *Homo erectus* (i.e. in Asia) than we can deduce archaeologically. The survival of Neanderthal man is still on the whole more plausible. Moreover the Almas' supposed inability to make fire is as much of a problem in connecting him with *Homo erectus* as it is with Neanderthal man. *Homo erectus* invented the use of fire.

Of the Chuchunaa we can say little. The region they inhabit, in eastern Siberia around Yakut, is one of the least explored areas in the world, and solid evidence is hard to come by. They differ from the Almas in being tall (over 6 ft 6 in.), wearing clothes and having the use of fire. Apart from their height, they might in fact make a better Neanderthal candidate than the Almas, but until we know more about them further speculation is pointless.

Where do we go from here? Both Yetis and Almas are still scientific anomalies and people observing them have to make a choice whether or not to believe the evidence of their own eyes and face possible ridicule and scepticism, or to conceal the experience until someone else has proved the existence of the phenomenon. Behaviourists call this problem 'cognitive dissonance', a lack of agreement between someone's perceptions and their experience, and its solution is not aided by the excessive press and media coverage given to hoaxes and fakes. It is undeniably true that some reports have been faked – the Iceman is a case in point and actual jokers with footprint machines have been caught – but many such hoaxes are likely to be exposed either at the time they happen or when a scientist analyzes their results in detail. It is impossible, for instance, to fake the weight distribution of a large primate as manifested in its footprint, and with each passing year we are gaining new information about primate anatomy.

Science decides what is real, giving contemporary science a role in society analogous to that held by the clergy in earlier times. Fortunately scientists have now realized that not all phenomena which at first seem puzzling need necessarily be fabricated – they may well be the result of previously unknown forces. Wildmen reports are no longer isolated occurrences; they can be correlated over wide areas and theories advanced concerning the classification, origin and lifestyles of these creatures. One carcass, just one, is all that is required for definitive proof. But what should be our policy in obtaining one? Is it ethical to shoot a Sasquatch for science? Dmitri Bayanov believes (and I agree with him) that it is morally unjustifiable to kill any hominid or related creature.[6] Different countries have protected their wildmen and prohibited their hunting, but if a Yeti presented itself conveniently in front of the sights of even the most ardent conservationist, would he not be tempted to pull the trigger?[7] The few specimens that have apparently been killed have usually evoked guilt because of their manlike appearance, giving the hunter the feeling that he has committed murder. Of course, the alternative to shooting an example is to set up long-term study projects in the field, with the observer blending in with the fauna, but such projects would be costly, lengthy and unspectacular, and in the current parlous state of most institutional sources of finance, impossible. *Anything* is better than killing a 'wildman' but would anything else convince the sceptics? Regrettably, I think not.

However, recent surveys have shown that perhaps the question doesn't matter anyway. In 1978 300 Canadian and American scientists were sent a questionnaire which dealt with their attitudes towards Bigfoot and the Loch Ness Monster.[8] Of these scientists 100 were physical anthropologists specializing in primatology and human evolution, and the rest acted as a control group. Half the total were sent a Bigfoot questionnaire, and 71 physical anthropologists responded. Of the 39 Bigfoot questionnaires thus obtained 13 per cent accepted him as an animal unknown to science (against 23 per cent for Nessie). The reasons against were:

| | per cent |
| --- | --- |
| Lack of fossil evidence | 46.2 |
| Lack of specimen (or parts of) | 74.4 |
| Lack of bones | 61.5 |
| Lack of nutritional sources in environment | 12.8 |
| Too tall/too large | 2.6 |
| Could not have remained so long undetected by science | 35.9 |
| Too bizarre to consider | 2.6 |

So it all boils down, as one might expect, to the lack of skeletal evidence. A further question showed that only 5 per cent believed that the discovery of Bigfoot would have a severe impact on science, and an (to me) astonishing 43 per cent thought that his discovery would be only moderately or slightly important. 61 per cent said that science should support Bigfoot research, but only half of these believed that government money should be used. The majority of those questioned had read at least some of the literature, and at least a third of the physical anthropologists had read John Napier's book on the subject (*Bigfoot*, 1972). Many people (40 per cent) believed that some of the Bigfoot reports involved sighting other animals, such as bears, and nearly 70 per cent suggested hoaxing. One could conclude, predictably, that there is a fair degree of scepticism about the existence of Bigfoot, but that this is mainly based on the lack of hard evidence, not doubts about ecological or evolutionary possibilities.

## Selected comments on Bigfoot by physical anthropologists[9]

1   There is an absence of physical evidence to support the existence of this hypothetical creature, and quite significant theoretical basis for doubting its existence. I can't take all the time *gratis* to go into all the details now ... but think that if you're really serious you might want to expend some of your own resources on an

effort to explore the reasons why a number of open-minded scientists with experience in the field doubt that this is a fruitful subject for investigation.

2   In that a lack of something can't be proved in the strict logical sense, I tell my students that it is far wiser to claim to believe [in Bigfoot] because if they don't exist, who's to prove you wrong?

3   I . . . consider it quite possible that an unknown-to-science large hominid may be living in Asia (but probably not in America).

4   There are some supposed observations which are obvious confusions; there is some purposeful fakery. But you cannot deny the hundreds of observations by reliable individuals who have nothing to gain by making such observations public, and you cannot deny the miles of footprints – often found in places where no one would be expected to make such footprints.

5   Although I feel this research would probably be a waste of time, I would never presume to say that anyone 'should not' do it – everyone should have the freedom to make an ass of himself, if that is what he wants.

6   I am doing it (Bigfoot research). I am a member of the National Academy of Sciences.

7   Until or unless there is more tangible evidence . . . it would be absurd for a sensible scientist to undertake or for federal funds to be devoted to such research. It does make some sense to investigate why so many people believe things without acceptable evidence, and I suppose that is what you are up to . . .

8   We lose 2/3 aircraft per year in the mountains here (Seattle). If we cannot find a large static object in forests, why is it not possible to have difficulty finding a moving, smaller object (especially if these are rare and attempting to avoid contact)?

Of course this survey refers only to the North American Bigfoot, and it would be most interesting to get some comparative data for Almas; information about them is unfortunately not nearly so easy to come by. What surprises me is that so many people think the question of whether or not such creatures exist, and what they are, is trivial. It would have immense repercussions in studies of primate evolution alone, to say nothing of its anthropological importance to the study of myths and folklore. I cannot believe that Yetis and Almas are purely creatures of my imagination, a hypothesis only plausible if there had never been any real wildmen. Even if you discount half the evidence you are still left with a substantial volume of material. I am ready to accept that people are capable of imagining things, perhaps even the same things – but imagination does not create unclassifiable footprints.

# Notes

## Prologue (pages 7–15)

1 Fiedler, L. (1981) *Freaks: Myths and images of the Secret Self*, London. This, the 'classic' work on the subject, has a rigorously critical approach and vast bibliography. 'Monsters' are discussed in detail by various authors in the first part of another book, Halpin, M. M. and Ames, M. (eds.) (1980) *Man-like Monsters on Trial*, Vancouver, which arose out of a conference on 'humanoid' monsters held at the University of British Columbia in 1976, organized by the senior author.

2 The original spelling is Neander*th*al not Neandertal. It has been said that this should be retained for *Homo sapiens neanderthalensis* but that changes in German orthography make the spelling Neandertal more correct. This has led to much confusion, and the original spelling is retained in this book.

3 Porshnev's other works include:
(1955) 'O drevneishem sposobe polucheniya ognya' ('On the most ancient means of obtaining fire'), *Sovetskaya etnografiya*, no. 1;
(1955) 'Novye dannye o vysekanii ognya' ('New data on making fire'), *Kratkie soobshcheniya Instituta etnografii*, vyp. XXIII, 3.
(1955) 'Materializm i idealizm v voprosakh stanovleniya cheloveka' ('Materialism and idealism in questions concerning the origin of man'), *Voprosy filosofii*, no. 5;
(1957) 'Esche k voprosu o stanovlenii cheloveka' ('More on the ques-
tion of the origin of man'), *Sovetskaya antropologiya*, no. 2;
(1958) 'K sporam o probleme vozniknoveniya chelovecheskogo obshchestva' ('Towards the debate on the problem of the rise of human society'), *Voprosy istorii*, no. 2;
(1958) 'Problema vozniknoveniya chelovecheskogo obshchestva i chelovecheskoi kul'tury' ('The problem of the rise of human society and human culture') *Vestnik istorii mirovoi kul'tury*, no. 2;
(1962) 'Sostoyanie pogranichnykh problem biologicheskikh i obshchestvenno-istoricheskikh nauk' ('The position of problems of demarcation between the biological and socio-historical sciences'), *Voprosy filosofii*, no. 5;
(1963) *Sovremennoe sostoyanie voprosa o reliktovykh gominoidakh* (*The current position with regard to the question of relict hominoids*), Moscow;
(1964) 'Rechepodrazhanie (ekholaliya) kak stupen' formirovaniya ztoroi signal'noi sistemy' ('Voice mimicry (echolalia) as a stage in the formation of a second signalling system'), *Voprosy psikhologii*, no. 5;
(1964) 'Lo stato attuale del problema degli ominoidi regregiti', *Genus*, vol. XX no. 1–4;
(1966) 'Vozmozhna li seichas nauchaya revolyutsiya v primatologii?' ('Is a scientific revolution in primatology now possible?') *Voprosy filosofii*, no. 3;
(1968) 'Antropogeneticheskie aspekty fiziologii vysshei nervnoi

deyatel'nosti i psikhologii' ('Anthropogenetic aspects of the physiology of higher nervous activity and psychology'), *Voprosy psikhologii*, no. 5;
(1968) 'Bor'ba za trogloditov' ('The struggle on behalf of troglodytes'), *Prostor*, Alma-Ata, nos. 4, 5, 6, 7;
(1971) 'Vtoraia signal'naia sistema kak diagnosticheskii rubezh mezhdu trogloditami i gominidami' ('The second signal system as a diagnostic line of distinction between the troglodytidae and the hominidae). *Doklady Akademia Nauk SSSR*, n.s. 198, no. 1, 228–31;
(1972) 'The Hominidae and the Troglodytae'. *Pursuit* 5, no. 1, 10–11;
(1974) 'The Troglodytae and the Hominidae in the Taxonomy and Evolution of Higher Primates' (with comments and reply), *Current Anthropology* 15, no. 4, 449–56.
4 The term Almas is used in this book as both singular and plural, for the sake of simplicity. However the literature tells us that the plural may also be Almasti, Almasy, Almas nar, Almases etc.
5 The whole Iceman question is discussed in detail by Bernard Heuvelmans in his half of Heuvelmans, B. and Porshnev, B. (1974) *L'homme de néanderthal est toujours vivant*, Paris.

### Chapter 1 (pages 16–33)

1 Beazley, J. D. (1956) *Attic Black-Figure Vase Painters*, and (1963) *Attic Red-Figure Vase Painters* (both Clarendon Press, Oxford) list all the themes, artists and available fragments with meticulous details and commentaries. They are the standard works of reference on the subject. For something a little lighter, see Boardman, J. (1974) *Athenian Black Figure Vases* and (1975) *Athenian Red Figure Vases* (both Thames and Hudson, London). These are much more readable.
2 Reinach, S. (1906) *Répertoire de la statuaire grécque et romaine*, vol. I, 2nd edition, Paris.
3 Boardman, J. *pers. comm.*
4 Graves, R. (1955) *The Greek Myths*, 2 vols, Harmondsworth.
5 Graves first produced this idea in his foreword to a revised edition of his *Greek Myths* (1955). It was elaborated in his book about poetic myth, *The White Goddess* (London, 1971). The use of hallucinogens in antiquity is now widely established from archaeological evidence – see references in my book *Environmental Archaeology* (London, 1981).
6 The source here is largely Bernheimer, R. (1952) *Wild Men in the Middle Ages*, Cambridge, Mass.
7 Lovejoy, A. and Boas, G. (1935) *Primitivism and related ideas in antiquity*, Baltimore.
8 Although this has been claimed by Porshnev (1974) *op. cit.* (Prologue note 3) and further discussed by Bayanov, D. and Burtsev, I. (1976) 'On Neanderthal vs *Paranthropus*', *Current Anthropology*, 17, no. 2, 312–18, which comments on Porshnev's work and reactions to it.
9 I am grateful to Claud Luttrell for this information.
10 Sanderson, I. T. (1967) 'The Wudewasa, or hairy primitives of ancient Europe', *Genus*, 23, nos, 1–2, 109–140. A fascinating and comprehensive account of the whole subject.
11 Smith, J. C. D. (1974) *A Guide to Church Woodcarving*, Newton Abbot. Has some splendid examples of greenmen.
12 Larwood, J. and Hotten, J. C. (1860) *Inn Signs*, London.
13 The bibliographies in Hitching, F. (1980) *The Pan Atlas of Mys-*

*teries*, London, are my source for most of the stories.

**14** Ogburn, W. F. (1956) wrote an amusing paper on 'The wolf boy of Agra' in *Am. Jnl. of Sociology* 64, and, with a colleague, tried to sift fact from fancy in a further article 'On the track of the wolf children', *Genetic Psychology Monographs* 60, 117–93, by Ogburn, W. F. and Bose, N. K. (1959). This latter work strongly attacked the best known account of these phenomena by Gesell, A. (1978) *Wolf Child and Human Child*, New York. The sources used by these writers include Kellog, W. N. (1931) 'More about the wolf children of India', *Am. Jnl. of Psychology* 43, and Singh, J. A. L. and Zagg R. M. (1942), *Wolf children and Feral Man*, New York.

**15** Quoted extensively, e.g. Bayanov and Burtsev (1976) *op. cit.* (note 8) p. 316. Original reference in Virey, J. J. (1817). *Nouvelle dictionnaire d'histoire naturelle*, Paris.

**16** Bayanov and Burtsev (1976) *op. cit.* (note 8) p. 316. Original reference p. 230 in Tajel, J. F. (1848) *Die fundamental philosophie in genetischer Entwicklung mit besordener Rücksicht auf die Geschichte jedes einzelnen Problems*, Tübingen.

**17** Dennis, W. (1941) 'The significance of feral man,' *Am. Jnl. of Psychology*, 54.

**18** Lane, H. (1977) *The Wild Boy of Aveyron*, London. A more recent account is Shattuck, R. (1980) *The Forbidden Experiment: the story of the Wild Boy of Aveyron*, London.

**19** Armen, Jean-Claud (1974) *Gazelle Boy*, London.

**20** E.g. Bettleheim, B. (1959) 'Feral Children and Autistic Children', *Am. Jnl. of Sociology*, 64, 455–67. This is the main work suggesting that feral children are probably severely retarded.

**21** Hitching, F. (1980) *The Pan*

*Atlas of Mysteries*, London.

**22** Originally quoted by Wagner, M. (1796) *Beitrage zür philosophischen Anthropologie und den damit Verwandten Wissenschaften*, 2 vols, Vienna.

**Chapter 2 (pages 34–51)**

**1** Napier, J. (1972) *Bigfoot: the Yeti and Sasquatch in Myth and Reality*, London. The best (and least sensationalized) account. See also Hunter, D. and Dahinden, R. (1973) *Sasquatch*, Toronto; Byrne, P. (1975) *The Search for Bigfoot: Monster, Myth or Man?*, New York; Sprague, R. and Krantz, G. S. (1977) *The Scientist looks at the Sasquatch*, Salt Lake City.

**2** Green, J. (1980) 'What is the Sasquatch?', in Halpin, M. and Ames, M. M. (eds.) *Manlike Monsters on Trial*, Vancouver, 237–45. His previous works form virtually a Bigfoot archive: (1967) Reports indicating the Existence of Giants, Human-like Creatures, in North America, and Comment Thereon', *Genus*, 23, nos. 3–4, 221–45; (1968) *On the track of the Sasquatch*, Agassiz, B. C.; (1970) *The Year of the Sasquatch*, Agassiz, B.C.; (1973) *The Sasquatch File*, Agassiz, B. C.; (1978) *Sasquatch: The Apes among us*, Saanichton, B. C.

**3** Byrne, P. (1980) 'The Elusive Yeti: Illusion or Elusion?' *Geographical Magazine*.

**4** Kerlin, R. L. and Hertel, L. (1980) 'Estimates of pitch and vocal tract length from recorded vocalizations of purported Bigfoot', in Halpin and Ames (eds.) *op. cit.* (note 2), 276–91.

**5** Bryant, V. M. and Trevor-Deutsch, B. (1980) 'Analysis of faeces and hair suspected to be of Sasquatch origin', in Halpin and Ames (eds.) *op. cit.* (note 2),

291–301.

6 For a comprehensive account of the method and theory of coprolite analysis see Shackley, M. L. (1981) *Environmental Archaeology*, London.

7 Published by Franklin Press, 1966, but mostly a collection of newspaper accounts with little comment.

8 A note by J. Beckford in *Current Anthropology*, 22, no. 1, 1981, 98, says that Patterson and Gimlin did not, as most people suppose, measure the tracks at the site themselves, but a man called Bob Titmus did this several days afterwards. Roger Patterson himself died in 1972.

9 Quoted in Hunter and Dahinden (1973) *op. cit.* (note 1).

10 Napier (1972) *op. cit.* (note 1), p. 102.

11 Gill, G. W. (1980) 'Population clines of the North American Sasquatch as evidenced by Track Lengths and Estimated Statures' in Halpin and Ames (eds.) *op. cit.* (note 2), 265–76. Anthropological studies of Sasquatch anatomy have also been undertaken by the eminent anthropologist Grover S. Krantz: (1971) 'Sasquatch Handprints', *Northwest Anthropological Research Notes*, 5, no. 2, 145–51; (1972) 'Anatomy of the Sasquatch Foot', *Northwest Anthrop. Research Notes*, 6, no. 1, 91–104; (1972) 'Additional Notes on Sasquatch Foot Anatomy', *Northwest Anthrop. Research Notes*, 6, no. 2, 230–41.

12 Dillon, L. S. (1973) *Evolution: Concepts and Consequences*, St Louis.

13 Coon, C. S. (1955) 'Some problems of human variability and natural selection in climate and culture', *American Naturalist*, 89, 257–80.

14 Claiborne, R. (1978) *The First American*, New York, gives a general account of the earliest colonization of North America and some geological background.

## Chapter 3 (pages 52–68)

1 Rawicz, S. (1956) *The Long Walk*, London.

2 Shipton, E. (1956) 'Fact or Fancy', *Geographical Journal*, 122 no. 3, 370–2.

3 See Shipton, E. (1952) *The Mount Everest Reconnaissance Expedition, 1951*, London; also Shipton, E. (1969) *That Untravelled World: an Autobiography*, London. For accounts of the conquest of Everest in 1953, see Hunt, J. (1953) *The Ascent of Everest*, London, and (1958) 'Memories of a Mountain Land', in Tchernine, O. (ed.) *Explorers' and Travellers' Tales*, London, 13–14. Aslo Tenzing, N. (1955) *Tiger of the Snows: the Autobiography of Tenzing of Everest*, New York (also published as *Tenzing, Tiger of Everest*), which reports finds of two Yeti skulls in 1955, and tracks in 1946 and 1952. Less well-known tracks are recorded in Tschernezky, W. and Cooke, C. R. (1975) 'Unpublished Tracks of Snowman or Yeti', *Mankind Quarterly*, 15, no. 3, 163–77.

4 Napier, J. (1972) *Bigfoot*, London.

5 Chronicled in Izzard, R. (1955) *The Abominable Snowman Adventure*, London, and Stonor, C. (1955) *The Sherpa and the Snowman*, London.

6 Stonor, C. (1955) *op. cit.*

7 I am greatly indebted to Gerhard Wagner for information about the role of wildmen in Tibetan art. Diligent search of the vast *thanka* collection of the British Museum and Victoria and Albert Museum did not, alas, produce a single example.

For general accounts of Tibetan art and religion see: Zwalf, W. (1981) *Heritage of Tibet*, London (an exhibition catalogue, but the best basic book on Tibetan art and religion available); Fürer-Haimendorf, C. von (1964) *The Sherpas of Nepal: Buddhist Highlanders*, London (use of Yeti cap in ceremonial dances); Nebesky-Wojkowitz, R. de (1956) *Oracles and Demons of Tibet: the Cult and Iconography of the Tibetan Protective Deities*, The Hague; David-Neel, A. (1967) *Magic and Mystery in Tibet*, London (a wonderful account, by the only English female lama).
8 Sanderson, I. T. (1961) *Abominable Snowman: Legend come to Life*, Philadelphia and New York.
9 Hunt, J. (1958) *op. cit.* (note 3).

### Chapter 4 (pages 77–90)

1 *Daily Telegraph*, 2 December 1980, by 'Our Staff Correspondent in Peking'.
2 Zhu, Shi (1977) 'You Yeren Ma?' ('Does the wildman exist?') *Huashi (Fossils)*, vol. 15.
3 Zhenxin, Yuan and Wanpo, Huang (1979) 'Wild Man – fact or fiction?' *China Reconstructs*, 28, 56–9; Zhi, Xiao (1979) 'Shennongjia Forests: home of rare species,' *China Reconstructs*, 27, 28–32.
4 Zhenxin, Yuan and Wanpo, Huang (1981) 'A Challenge to Science: The Mystery of the Wildmen', in *Fortean Times* Occasional Paper No. 1, entitled *Wild Man. China's Yeti*, 5–15. A monograph containing reprints of several articles on this theme. This article was originally published in *Huashi*, 19 (1979), no. 1.
5 Jingguan, Fan (1980) 'He "yeren" mu zi xiangyu zai lishu lin' ('An encounter with a "wildman"

mother and child in the chestnut forest'), *Huashi*, 23, no. 1 reprinted in the *Fortean Times* monograph, 15–27.
6 Quoted by Zhenxin and Wanpo (1979) *op. cit.* (note 4).
7 I am indebted to Charles Aylmer for translating this article from the Chinese.
8 According to Zhenxin and Wanpo (1979) *op. cit.* (note 4).
9 The best (but not uncontested) overviews of these early stages of human evolution are those of Richard Leakey in his books (1979) *Origins*, London and New York; and (1980) *The Making of Mankind*, London and New York.
10 Le Cros Clark, W. (1978) *The Fossil Evidence for Human Evolution*, 3rd edition, Chicago; Eckhart, R. B. (1975) 'Gigantopithecus as a Hominid', in Tuttle, R. (ed.) *Palaeoanthropology, morphology and paleoecology*, The Hague, 105–29; Frayer, D. W. (1979) 'Gigantopithecus and its relationship to Australopithecus', *Am. J. Phys. Anthropol.* 39, 413–26.

### Chapter 5 (pages 91–108)

1 I was told this story by Dmitri Bayanov of the Darwin Museum, Moscow, who heard it first-hand from Ivlov himself. The Russians believe it implicitly.
2 Rinchen, V. (1964) 'Almas still exists in Mongolia', *Genus*, 20, 186–92. The only work of his available in English (of a sort), with many firsthand accounts and much folkloric detail. Another précis of his work may be found in 'Almasi, Mongolia's parent of the Snowman' (in Russian), *Sovremensaya Mongolia* (1958), 534–8.
3 In contrast to the Yeti, which is frequently greatly feared.
4 Although Schiltberger's work

has been quoted before, this account and manuscript work were kindly brought to my attention by Gerhard Wagner.

5 Extract from 'Hans Schiltberger's Journey into Heathen Parts', original in the Manuscripts Department of the Municipal Library in Munich, Sign. L1603 Bl. 210. Translated from the German by David Parsons.

6 Vlček, E. (1959) 'Old Literary evidence for the existence of the "Snowman" in Tibet and Mongolia', *Man*, 59, 133–4. Further comments on the translations were given by the same author in a later (1960) paper ('Diagnosis of the "wild man" according to Buddhist literary sources from Tibet, Mongolia and China', *Man*, 60, 153–4).

7 Different books give Rinchen different initials (e.g. Tchernine calls him *J. R.* Rinchen, Vlček (1959, 1960) *B.* Rinchen, and the definitive work of Rupen, R. A. (1964) *Mongols of the Twentieth Century*, Bloomington, Indiana, lists his known works and gives his last name as Rincen, although his first name is listed elsewhere as Yöngsiyebiü.

8 Christopher Dobson, in the *Daily Express*, 30 July 1959.

9 Zhamtsarano's scholarly works include (1955) *The Mongol Chronicles of the Seventeenth Century*, trans. R. Loewenthal, Wiesbaden.

10 T. Ts. Tudenova O fonde Ts. Zh. Zhamtsarano. Trudy Bion BF. So. An. SSSR. 1969 (12) 138–142. '*Materialypo istomi i filologii Tsentral'noi A2ii*' (in Russian), 4, which says that the Zhamtsarano archive at Ulan Ude contains not only many personal details about the man but also his field notes for various trips between 1904 and 1909. Like all these Russian bibliographic references, this is the work of Michael Heaney.

11 Also known as *Leningradshoe otdelenie Institut a vostokove-*

*deniya Akademii nank SSSR*, collection no. 62, dating 1903–36.

12 *Institut obshchestvennykh nank Buryatskogo filiala sibirskogo otdeleniya Akademii nank SSSR*, collection no. 6, items dated between 1890 and 1917 and housed at Ulan Ude.

13 E.g. The descriptions of Mongolia published in the *Uchenye zapiski Institut Vostokovedeniya AN SSSR*, 6 (1953), 35–53 and 9 (1954), 90–127.

14 This list appears in *Central Asiatic Journal*, 4–3 (1959), 199–206. 'L'héritage scientifique du Prof. dr. Zamcarano.' (List in Russian, text in French.)

15 'The Passage of Almas', by M. Rosenfeld, 1936, in Heuvelmans and Porshnev (1974), *op. cit.*, 40.

16 Bannikov, A. G. (1976) 'Wild camels of the Gobi', *Wildlife*, 18, no. 9, 398–403.

17 Rinchen – see note 2 above.

18 General article called 'Again the Snowman' in *Mongolie*, 6 (1980), 24. An illustrated bi-monthly magazine published in Ulan Bator, not widely available.

## Chapter 6 (pages 109–16)

1 Satunin, K. A. (1899) 'Biabanguli', *Priroda i okhota (Nature and Hunting)* 7, 28–35 (in Russian, translated by Michael Heaney). A prosaic account by the renowned naturalist.

2 Porshnev, B. (1969) 'Problema reliktovykh paleoantropov' ('The Problem of Relic Paleoanthropines'), *Sovetskaya etnografiya*, 2, 115–30 (in Russian, translated by Michael Heaney).

3 Colarusso, J. (1980) 'Ethnographic information on a wild man of the Caucasus', in Halpin and Ames (eds.) (1980), 255–65.

4 Bayanov, D. (1981) 'On the trail

– journey of a researcher', *Bigfoot Co-operative*, 2, 9–10.

5 Biographical details about the redoubtable Dr Kofman are from Heuvelmans and Porshnev (1974).

6 Kofman, Zh. I. (1968) 'Otvet professoru Avdeevu' ('Reply to Professor Avdeev'), *Nauka i religiya*, no. 4, 'Sledy ostayutsya. . . .' ('The tracks remain. . . .').

7 See note 4.

8 Note of sightings made by Khazkisuv Khutov in *Bigfoot Co-operative*, 2 (1981), 9.

## Chapter 7 (pages 117–26)

1 Dravert, P. (1933) 'Dikie lyndi muleny i chuchuna' ('The wild mulen and chuchuna people'), *Buduschaya Subir*, 6 (40–43) (in Russian).

2 Zerchaninov, Yu, (1980) 'Riskni uvidet' ('Dare to see'), *Yunost*, 3, 106–9 (in Russian).

3 Pronin, A. G. (1958) ' "Abominable Snowman" in the Pamirs?', *Moscow News*, 23 January, 3.

4 Porshnev, B. (1969) 'Problema reliktovykh paleoantropov' ('The Problem of Relict Paleoanthropines'), *Sovetskaya etnografiya*, 2, 115–30.

5 Stanyukovitch, K. V. (1965) *Po sledam udivitel'noi zagadki* (*On the trail of an amazing mystery*), Moscow; Bianki V. L. (1961) 'Pro snezhnogo cheloveka' ('About the Snowman') *Priklyu-cheniya v gorakh*, Book I, Moscow. A brief account also appears in *Izvestia*, 9 January 1960, also by Stanyukovitch.

6 Tchernine, O. (1961) *The Snowman and Company*, London.

7 Pemnova, R. (1958) 'Che poveyeer, komorvii elo videl . . .', *Vokrugsvieta*, 12, 34–9.

8 Account translated by Dmitri Bayanov in *Bigfoot Co-operative*,
2, June 1981.

9 Bayanov, D. (1981) 'Expedition "Gissar" – 80', *Bigfoot Co-operative*, 2, August.

10 Zasseda, I. (1981) ' "L'homme des neiges" dans les montagnes du Tadjikstan?', *Les Nouvelles de Moscow*, 46, 15 October, 10.

## Chapter 8 (pages 127–39)

All translations from the Russian in this chapter are by Michael Heaney.

1 Pushkarev, V. (1978) 'Nevye Svidetel'stra' ('New Testimony'), *Tekhnika molodezhi*, 6, 48–52 (in Russian). Vladimir Pushkarev, who ought to have known better, ignored all basic survival training and set out alone on a long hiking and boating journey through the Siberian taiga in 1978, never to return.

2 Burtseva, A. (1978) 'Zolotoi sled na Chukotke' ('Golden trail in Chukotka'), *Tekhnika molodezhi*, 6, 52–3.

3 Name variants Chuchunaa, Suchunaa, Kuchunaa, Chuchuna etc. are all used for these manlike creatures.

4 See note 1.

5 Dravert, P. (1933) 'Dikie lyudi muleny i chuchuna' ('The wild mulen and chuchunaa people'), *Budushchaya Sibir*, 6, 40–3 (in Russian). Dravert made a preliminary announcement of his collections of Chuchunaa stories in 1912, using them as an introductory episode to a piece of his work that was printed in a Kazan newspaper (Dravert, P. (1912) 'Na sevene dal'nem' ('In the Far North'), *Kamskorolzhskaya rech*, no. 239).

6 See Dravert (1933), *op. cit.* (note 5).

7 *Istoricheskie predaniya i rasskazy yakutov* (*Historical legends and tales of the Yakuts*), publication prepared by G. U. Ergis

under the editorship of A. A. Popov, part 1, Moscow and Leningrad 1960 (Academy of Sciences of the USSR, Yakut branch of the Siberian section, Institute of Language, Literature and History). Texts in Yakut and Russian.

### Chapter 9 (pages 140–64)

1 All this is highly controversial. See Leakey (1981) *The Making of Mankind*, London and New York, for a balanced (if superficial) view, or Shackley, M. L. (1980) *Neanderthal Man*, London.
2 Gerasimov, M. (1971) *The Face Finder*, trans. A. H. Brodrick, London.
3 See Napier, J. (1972) *Bigfoot*, London, for a comparison of Neanderthal and Yeti footprints.
4 This whole question is considered by Krantz, G. S. (1980) 'Sapienization and speech', *Current Anthropology*, 21, no. 6, 773–92, with a very extensive discussion and bibliography.
5 Stringer, C. B. (1974) 'Population relationships of late Pleistocene hominids: a multivariate study of available crania', *Journal of Archaeological Science*, 1, 317–42.
6 All these arguments are discussed in Shackley, M. L. (1982) 'The case for neanderthal survival; fact, fiction and faction', *Antiquity*, LVI, no. 216, 31–41.
7 Thanks are due to the British Council, the University of Ulan Bator and the British Embassy (Ulan Bator) for help with this trip.
8 This work will shortly be fully published but an abstract has already appeared in the 1982 Book of Abstracts of the XIth INQUA Conference (Session 29) held in Moscow, 1–9 August 1982, vol. 2, p. 287.

### Epilogue (pages 165–76)

1 *New Scientist*, 12 March 1981, 695.
2 Heuvelmans, B. (1963) *On the Track of Unknown Animals*, London.
3 This controversy has been the subject of a spirited correspondence in *Nature, New Scientist* etc. and of a BBC Horizon documentary called 'Did Darwin get it Wrong?'. The consensus was that he didn't.
4 For an example of two conflicting views of the early beginnings of the hominid story, see: Leakey R. (1981) *The Making of Mankind*, London and New York; and Johannsen, D. (1981) *Lucy: The Beginnings of Humankind*, New York and London.
5 I am indebted to Dr H. H. E. Loofs-Wissowa, Australian National University, for this information.
6 The arguments about killing hominids have been summed up by Austin, E. and Padmore, T. (1978) 'Sasquatch: The Sceptics want Corpse', *Vancouver Sun*, 15 May, 26; Bayanov, D. (1980) 'Why it is not right to kill a gentle giant', *Pursuit*, Autumn, 40–1, where he makes a rebuttal of the conclusions reached by John Green in Green, J. (1978) *Sasquatch: The Apes Among Us*, Seattle.
7 Matthiessen, in *The Snow Leopard* (1979) comments on this dilemma. One of the participants in the Arun Valley expedition actually had a permit to 'collect' a Yeti, but had not, apparently, decided whether it was morally justifiable to do so.
8 Greenwell, J. R. and King, J. E. (1980) 'Scientists and anomalous phenomena: preliminary result of a survey', *Zetetic Scholar 6*, Dept. of Sociology, Eastern Michigan University: whose conclusions are summarized in Greenwell, J. R. and

King, J. E. (1981) 'Attitudes of Physical Anthropologists towards reports of Bigfoot and Nessie', *Current Anthropology*, 22 (i), 79–80.

9 Quoted in Greenwell and King (1980) *op. cit.*

# Further Reading

The reader who wants to consider detailed points should refer to the Notes.

The following is a brief list of general works:

BERNHEIMER, R. (1952) *Wild Men in the Middle Ages*, Cambridge, Mass.

BORD, J. AND C. (1982) *Bigfoot*, London.

FIEDLER, L. (1981) *Freaks, Myths and Images of the Secret Self*, Harmondsworth.

HALPIN, M. M. AND AMES, M. (eds.) (1980) *Manlike Monsters on Trial*, Vancouver.

HEUVELMANS, B. (1962) *On the Track of Unknown Animals*, London.

HEUVELMANS, B. AND PORSHNEV, B. (1974) *L'homme de néanderthal est toujours vivant*, Paris.

HITCHING, F. (1980) *The Pan Atlas of Mysteries*, London.

IZZARD, R. (1955) *The Abominable Snowman Adventure*, London.

MICHELL, J. AND RICKARD, R. J. M. (1977) *Phenomena*, London and New York.

(1982) *Living Wonders*, London and New York.

NAPIER, J. (1972) *Bigfoot: the Yeti and Sasquatch in Myth and Reality*, London.

SANDERSON, I. T. (1961) *Abominable Snowman: legend come to life*, Philadelphia and New York.

SHACKLEY, M. L. (1980) *Neanderthal Man*, London.

(1982) 'The Case for Neanderthal Survival: Fact, Fiction or Faction?' *Antiquity* LVI. no. 216, pp. 31–41.

STONOR, C. (1955) *The Sherpa and the Snowman*, London.

TCHERNINE, O. (1961) *The Snowman and Company*, London.

(1970) *The Yeti*, London.

# Acknowledgments

I gladly acknowledge a great debt to my friend Michael Heaney of the Bodleian Library, Oxford, not only for his painstaking translations of much of my source material from its original Russian, but also for a constant stream of ideas, enthusiasms and encouragement.

The forbearance of my colleagues Claud Luttrell, Charles Phythian-Adams, Michael Greenhalgh, Allan Mills and Professor W. Sluckin has been much appreciated when 'wildmen' veered into their own particular fields of interest. Mention must also be made of the gallant efforts of our Inter-Library Loan staff who coped admirably with requests for very strange material in diverse languages. My meetings and voluminous correspondence with Dmitri Bayanov (Darwin Museum, Moscow) have enabled me to obtain first-hand accounts of recent Russian happenings, and I am also indebted to Gerhard Wagner (Munich) for informative Tibetological discussions about Yetis. Charles Aylmer kindly translated some recent Chinese reports for me, and Professor Glyn Daniel made me feel respectable with an invitation to lecture in Cambridge. Marius Cooke, Liz Birkett, Vincent Megaw, Odette Tchernine, Rene Dahinden, Lord John Hunt, Steven Thornett, Dorothy Tudor, Elizabeth Moignard, John Boardman and John Napier were all instrumental in helping me complete this book in their various ways.

The maps and majority of the line drawings are by Elizabeth Birkett. Other figures are by courtesy of: Fig. 2 Ivan T. Sanderson; Fig. 7 Metropolitan Museum of Art, Harris Brisbane Dick Fund 1926, New York; Fig. 11 After Tschernezky; Figs. 13, 14 After *Hua Shi* and *Fortean Times*; Fig. 15 Robert Harding Associates; Figs. 19, 20 Georgie Glen after Khakhlov; Fig. 25 After Wood; Fig. 26 Giovanni Caselli.

Plates 6, 22, 23 and 27 are by the author. Others are by courtesy of: 1 Boston, Museum of Fine Arts 76.46; 2 Musée du Louvre, MNB 2774; 3 Darwin Museum, Moscow; 4 The Governing Body of Christ Church, Oxford; 5 Stadtbibliothek Nürnberg; 7 Bayerische Staatsbibliothek, Munich; 8 John Green; 9 Syndication International Ltd; 10–13 Rene Dahinden/Fortean Picture Library; 14, 15 Royal Geographical Society; 16 Mount Everest Foundation; 17 Royal Geographical Society; 18 Gordon Wiltsie/ Courtesy Outside Magazine; 19 Dr Zhou Guoxing/Fortean Picture Library; 20 *Fortean Times*; 21 John Reader and Prof. G. von Koenigswald; 24, 26 Royal Geographical Society; 25 Rene Dahinden/Fortean Picture Library; 28 Dmitri Bayanov; 29 Bertelsmann Verlag; 30 Dr F. Krantz, Rheinisches Mineralien-Kontor KG; 32 British Museum (Natural History); 33 Dr John Napier.

# Index